I0490534

BUSINESS DEVELOPMENT AND GROWTH HACK

FOR SMALL BUSINESSES AND START-UPS

Sangati Jagan Mohan Reddy

Copyright © Sangati Jagan Mohan Reddy
All Rights Reserved.

This book has been self-published with all reasonable efforts taken to make the material error-free by the author. No part of this book shall be used, reproduced in any manner whatsoever without written permission from the author, except in the case of brief quotations embodied in critical articles and reviews.

The Author of this book is solely responsible and liable for its content including but not limited to the views, representations, descriptions, statements, information, opinions and references ["Content"]. The Content of this book shall not constitute or be construed or deemed to reflect the opinion or expression of the Publisher or Editor. Neither the Publisher nor Editor endorse or approve the Content of this book or guarantee the reliability, accuracy or completeness of the Content published herein and do not make any representations or warranties of any kind, express or implied, including but not limited to the implied warranties of merchantability, fitness for a particular purpose. The Publisher and Editor shall not be liable whatsoever for any errors, omissions, whether such errors or omissions result from negligence, accident, or any other cause or claims for loss or damages of any kind, including without limitation, indirect or consequential loss or damage arising out of use, inability to use, or about the reliability, accuracy or sufficiency of the information contained in this book.

To all the Start-up entrepreneurs and small business owners out there,

This book is dedicated to you. You have the courage and determination to take risks and create something from nothing. Your hard work and dedication to your businesses are an inspiration to us all. May this book help you to develop your business and reach your goals.

Sincerely,

Sangati Jagan Mohan Reddy

Perseverance

Determination

Foreword

Preface

Acknowledgements

Prologue

Perseverance

YS Jagan Mohn Reddy

YS Jagan Mohan Reddy, Chief Minister of Andhra Pradesh is known for his significant contributions to the business development and startup ecosystem of Andhra Pradesh. He has been a leader who has shown great perseverance in the face of adversity and has worked hard to ensure that the state's development is on track.

Determination

Biyyapu Madhu Sudhan Reddy

Biyyapu Madhusudhan Reddy, Member of Legislative Assembly (MLA) from the SriKalahasti constituency is a strong advocate for the development of the startup ecosystem and business development. He has worked tirelessly to create an environment that is conducive to the growth and success of startups and business ventures . He is also a mentor and advisor to many startups, providing guidance and support to help them reach their goals through various government intiatives. His commitment to make a difference in the lives of entrepreneurs is commendable and his contribution to the startup ecosystem is invaluable. He is a true example of determination and hard work.

Foreword

It is my pleasure to write a foreword for this book, which is about business development for small businesses and start-ups. As the world of business continues to evolve and change, it is essential for small business owners and start-up entrepreneurs to stay ahead of the curve and stay competitive. This book provides invaluable insights and strategies for developing and growing a small business or start-up.

This book is written by a highly experienced business consultant who has knowledge and expertise in the field of business development is evident throughout the book. He provides practical advice and guidance on how to create a successful business plan, develop a strong marketing strategy, and create a competitive advantage. He also offers valuable insights on how to manage finances, attract investors, and build a strong business.

This book is an essential resource for any entrepreneur or small business owner or start-ups looking to take their business to the next level. It is filled with useful information and strategies that can help entrepreneurs and small business owners make the most of their business opportunities. I highly recommend this book to anyone looking to develop and grow their business.

Preface

This book is designed to help small business owners and start-ups develop their businesses. It provides a comprehensive overview of the key aspects of business development, from setting up a business to managing its growth to the marketing and sales strategies needed to succeed.

The book is written in a straightforward and easy-to-understand style, making it accessible to readers of all levels of experience. It is divided into sections that cover the different stages of business development, from the initial planning stages to the growth and expansion of the business. Each section includes practical advice and tips on how to make the most of the opportunities available.

The book is aimed at small business owners and start-ups who are looking to develop their businesses. It is also suitable for those who are considering starting a business, as well as those who are already in the process of setting up their business.

This book is the result of years of research and experience in the field of business development. It is based on the knowledge and insights of experienced business owners, entrepreneurs, and experts in the field. It is my hope that this book will provide readers with the information and guidance they need to develop their businesses and achieve success.

Acknowledgements

I would like to thank my Business Associates and partners for their invaluable guidance and support throughout the writing process. Their insights and expertise helped shape this book into the final product it is today.

I would also like to thank my wife, my kids, my family, friends and relatives for their unwavering support and encouragement. Without their love and understanding, this book would not have been possible.

I am also grateful to the Small Business Owners and Start-ups who shared their stories and experiences with me. Their willingness to open up and share their journeys was invaluable to this book.

Finally, I would like to thank all the readers who have taken the time to read this book. I hope it helps you in your business development journey.

Prologue

The world of business is ever-changing and evolving, and the success of any business depends on its ability to stay ahead of the curve. For small businesses and start-ups, this can be a daunting task. With limited resources and a lack of experience, it can be difficult to know where to start.

This book is designed to provide small business owners and start-ups with the tools and knowledge they need to develop their business and achieve success. It covers a wide range of topics, from marketing and finance to operations and customer service, and provides practical advice on how to create and maintain a successful business.

Whether you are just starting out or have been in business for years, this book will provide you with the insights and strategies you need to take your business to the next level. With the right knowledge and dedication, you can create a thriving business that will stand the test of time.

The book is written for entrepreneurs and small business owners who are looking to take their business to the next level. It is designed to be a comprehensive resource that can be used to develop a business plan, identify opportunities, and create a roadmap for success.

CHAPTER ONE

What is Business Development?

Business development is the process of growing a business by identifying and capitalizing on opportunities to increase sales, expand into new markets, and develop new products or services. It involves a wide range of activities, such as market research, strategic planning, product development, sales and marketing, and customer service. Business development is an important part of any business, as it helps to ensure that the company is able to remain competitive and profitable in the long term.

Business development is a broad term that encompasses many different activities. It involves developing new products or services, expanding into new markets, or improving existing products or services. It also involves identifying and capitalizing on opportunities to increase sales, such as through strategic partnerships, marketing campaigns, or new customer acquisition. Business development is a continuous process, as companies must constantly evaluate their strategies and adjust them to meet changing market conditions.

Business development is often seen as a strategic process, as it involves making decisions about the future of the company. It requires a thorough understanding of the company's strengths and weaknesses, as well as an understanding of the competitive landscape. Companies must also have a clear vision of where they want to go and how they plan to get there.

Business development is also a process of innovation. Companies must constantly look for new ways to improve their products or services, or to develop new ones. This requires a deep understanding of customer needs and the ability to develop creative solutions to meet those needs.

Business development is a complex process that requires a great deal of planning and execution. Companies must be willing to invest time and resources into the process in order to ensure success. It is also important to have a team of experienced professionals who help us guide the company

CHAPTER TWO

Establish a Clear Mission and Vision

Establishing a clear mission and vision for business development is essential for any business. A mission and vision statement provide a roadmap for the future of the business, outlining the goals and objectives that need to be achieved in order to be successful. They also provide a sense of purpose and direction for employees, customers, and stakeholders.

- The first step in establishing a clear mission and vision for business development is to define the company's purpose. This should include a statement of why the company exists, what it hopes to achieve, and how it plans to do so. This statement should be concise and easy to understand, while also conveying the company's core values and beliefs.

- The next step is to identify the company's core competencies. This should include the skills, knowledge, and resources that the company has to offer. This will help to define the company's competitive advantage and will also help to guide the development of the company's strategy.

- The third step is to set goals and objectives. These should be specific, measurable, achievable, relevant, and time-bound. They should also be aligned with the company's mission and vision. Goals and objectives should be regularly reviewed and updated to ensure that they remain relevant and achievable.

- The fourth step is to develop a strategy. This should include a detailed plan of action that outlines how the company will achieve its goals and objectives. It should also include a timeline for implementation and a budget for resources.

- The fifth step is to communicate the mission and vision to all stakeholders. This should include employees, customers, suppliers, and investors. It is important to ensure that everyone understands the company

CHAPTER THREE

Develop a Comprehensive Business Plan

A comprehensive business plan is a document that outlines the strategy and objectives of a business. It is a road map for the future of the business, and it serves as a guide for decision-making. A comprehensive business plan should include an executive summary, a market analysis, a competitive analysis, a financial plan, and an operational plan.

The executive summary is the first section of the business plan and should provide a brief overview of the business. It should include the company's mission statement, a description of the products or services offered, and the target market.

The market analysis should include an assessment of the current market, an analysis of the competition, and a description of the target market. It should also include an analysis of the industry trends and a description of the marketing strategy.

The competitive analysis should include an analysis of the strengths and weaknesses of the competition and a description of how the company plans to differentiate itself from the competition.

The financial plan should include a description of the company's financial goals and objectives, a description of the capital structure, and a description of the financial projections.

The operational plan should include a description of the company's operations, a description of the management team, and a description of the operational processes.

A comprehensive business plan should also include an appendix with supporting documents such as financial statements, market research, and customer surveys. The business plan should be reviewed and updated regularly to ensure that it is up-to-date and reflects the current business environment.

CHAPTER FOUR

Identify Target Markets and Customers

Identifying target markets and customers in business development is an important step in the process of launching a new product or service. It involves researching the needs of potential customers and understanding the competitive landscape. The goal is to identify the most profitable and viable markets for your product or service.

- **Conduct Market Research**: The first step in identifying target markets and customers is to conduct market research. This involves gathering data about the size and characteristics of the target market, the competitive landscape, and the customer's needs and preferences. This research shall be done through surveys, interviews, focus groups, and other methods.

- **Analyze the Data**: Once the data has been collected, it must be analyzed to identify potential target markets and customers. This involves looking at the data to determine what types of customers are most likely to be interested in the product or service, what their needs and preferences are, and what the competitive landscape looks like.

- **Develop a Profile**: Once the data has been analyzed, it is important to develop a profile of the target market and customers. This profile should include demographic information, such as age, gender, income level, and location. It should also include psychographic information, such as lifestyle, interests, and values.

- **Identify Opportunities**: Once the target market and customer profile have been developed, it is important to identify potential opportunities for the product or service. This involves looking at the competitive landscape to identify areas where the product or services are differentiated and where there is potential for growth.

- **Develop a Strategy**: Once the opportunities have been identified, it is important to develop a strategy for reaching the target market and customers.

CHAPTER FIVE

Research Competitors and Industry Trends

Researching competitors and industry trends is an important part of business development. It helps businesses to identify opportunities, stay ahead of the competition, and develop strategies to increase their market share. By taking the time to research and analyze competitors and industry trends, businesses gain a competitive edge and increase their chances of success.

- **Identify Competitors**: The first step in researching competitors and industry trends is to identify who your competitors are. This is done by researching the industry and looking for companies that offer similar products or services. You can also use online tools and Market Research to find out who your competitors are.

- **Analyze Competitors**: Once you have identified your competitors, the next step is to analyze their strategies. Look at their website, social media presence, and any other marketing materials they have.

This will give you an idea of their target market, pricing strategy, and other factors that help you develop a competitive strategy.

- **Monitor Industry Trends**: It's important to stay up to date on industry trends. This is done by reading industry publications, attending trade shows, and networking with other industry professionals. You should also attend industry events and conferences to stay informed about the latest developments in the industry. This will help you identify new opportunities and stay ahead of the competition.

- **Develop Strategies**: Once you have identified your competitors and monitored industry trends, the next step is to develop strategies to increase your market share. This includes developing new products or services, expanding into new markets, or improving your existing products and services.

- **Analyze Your Own Performance**: In addition to researching your competitors and industry trends, you should also analyze your own performance. This should be done by looking at your sales figures, customer feedback, and other data points. This will help you identify

areas   for   improvement   and
opportunities for growth.

CHAPTER SIX

Develop a Marketing Strategy

Developing a marketing strategy for business development is an essential part of any successful business. A marketing strategy is a plan of action that outlines how a business will reach its goals and objectives. It is a comprehensive plan that includes market research, product development, pricing, promotion, distribution, and customer service.

The first step in developing a marketing strategy is to identify the target market. This involves researching the target market to understand their needs, wants, and preferences. Once the target market is identified, the next step is to develop a product or service that meets the needs of the target market. This involves researching the competition and developing a unique product or service that will differentiate the business from its competitors.

The next step is to determine the pricing strategy. This involves researching the competition and determining the best pricing strategy to maximize profits. The pricing strategy should also take into account the cost of production and the cost of marketing.

The next step is to develop a promotional strategy. This involves creating a marketing plan that outlines how the business will reach its target market. This includes developing a website, creating advertising campaigns, and utilizing social media.

The final step is to develop a distribution strategy. This involves determining the best way to get the product or service to the target market. This could include utilizing a distribution network, direct sales, or a combination of both.

Developing a marketing strategy for business development is a complex process that requires research, planning, and implementation. It is important to understand the target market, develop a unique product or service, determine the best pricing strategy, create a promotional strategy, and develop a distribution strategy. By following these steps, businesses ensure that their marketing strategy is effective.

CHAPTER SEVEN

Develop a Promotional Strategy

A promotional strategy is a plan of action that businesses use to increase awareness of their products and services, build customer loyalty, and generate more sales. It involves a combination of marketing tactics such as advertising, public relations, social media, and other activities.

The impact of a promotional strategy on business development for small businesses and start-ups is very significant to create brand recognition, attract new customers, and increasing sales. It helps to build relationships with existing customers and create a positive reputation for the business to increase visibility and reach potential customers, which leads to more sales. It will help to create a competitive edge in the market, as well as help to differentiate the business from its competitors.

- **Identify Your Target Audience**: The first step in developing a promotional strategy is to identify your target audience. This means understanding who your customers are, what their needs and wants are, and how you can best reach them.

- **Set Goals and Objectives**: Once you've identified your target audience, you need to set goals and objectives for your promotional strategy. This will help you focus your efforts and ensure that you're working towards a clear end goal.

- **Choose the Right Channels**: Once you've identified your target audience and set goals and objectives, you need to decide which channels you'll use to reach them. This could include social media, email, print, radio, television, or any other medium.

- **Develop Your Message**: Once you've chosen the right channels, you need to develop your message. This should be tailored to your target audience and should clearly communicate the benefits of your product or service.

- **Track and Measure Results**: You need to track and measure the results of your promotional strategy. This will help you understand what's working and what's not, so you have to adjust your strategy accordingly.

By following these steps, you will develop an effective promotional strategy that will help you reach your business goals.

CHAPTER EIGHT

Develop a Distribution Strategy

Distribution strategies for business development are methods used to get products and services to the market. These strategies can be used to increase sales, reach new customers, and build brand awareness.

- **Direct Distribution**: Direct distribution is when a company sells its products directly to customers. This is done through a company's own website, retail stores, or through third-party websites like Amazon.

- **Indirect Distribution**: Indirect distribution is when a company uses a third party to distribute its products. This could be a wholesaler, distributor, or retailer.

- **Multi-Channel Distribution**: Multi-channel distribution is when a company uses multiple distribution channels to reach customers. This could include a combination of direct and indirect distribution, as well as online and offline channels.

- **Franchising:** Franchising is when a company allows other businesses to use its brand name and products. This is an intelligent way to expand a business quickly and reach new markets.

- **Licensing**: Licensing is when a company grants another company the right to use its products or services. This is often used when a company wants to expand into a new market or industry.

To implement these strategies, companies should identify their target markets and develop a plan to reach them. Companies should also consider their budget and resources when selecting a distribution strategy. Companies should monitor their distribution channels to ensure they are meeting customer needs and expectations.

CHAPTER NINE

Distribution Strategies

Direct Selling

Direct selling is a form of marketing in which a company sells products directly to consumers, usually in their own homes or through parties, rather than through a retail store. Direct selling is the best way to increase sales and grow a business. It allows companies to reach more potential customers, build relationships with customers, and increase brand awareness. It also allows companies to reduce overhead costs associated with traditional retail stores. Direct selling also helps companies increase their customer base and create loyal customers.

Direct selling is a type of business model in which goods and services are sold directly to consumers away from a fixed retail location. It is a form of business that has been around for centuries and is still popular today. Direct selling is often associated with door-to-door sales, but it also includes selling products through catalogs, parties, and online.

Direct selling has a number of advantages for businesses. It allows companies to reach a larger audience, build relationships with customers, and provide personalized service. It also provides an opportunity to test new products and services without investing in a large-scale marketing campaign.

The impact of direct selling on business growth is significant. It will help businesses reach new customers, increase sales, and build brand loyalty. It also helps businesses reduce costs associated with traditional marketing efforts. Direct selling helps businesses gain valuable customer insights that can be used to improve products and services.

Direct selling also helps to build relationships with customers. By engaging with customers directly, businesses can gain valuable feedback and insights that are to be used to improve products and services. Direct selling helps businesses build trust with customers, which can lead to increased sales and customer loyalty.

It is important to remember that direct selling is not a one-size-fits-all solution and should be tailored to the needs of the business.

Online Advertising

Online advertising is a form of marketing that uses the internet to deliver promotional messages to potential customers. It includes a variety of techniques, such as search engine optimization (SEO), pay-per-click (PPC) advertising, display advertising, and social media marketing. Online advertising has become an essential part of any successful business's marketing strategy.

The impact of online advertising on business growth

is undeniable. It allows businesses to reach a much wider audience than traditional advertising methods, such as television, radio, and print. Online advertising is much more cost effective than traditional advertising, as it requires fewer resources and can be targeted to specific audiences.

Online advertising help businesses increase brand awareness, generate leads, and increase sales. It also helps businesses build relationships with their customers and create loyalty. Online advertising help businesses track and measure the success of their campaigns, allowing them to make informed decisions about their marketing strategies.

Online advertising also has the potential to reach a global audience. This is especially beneficial for businesses that are targeting international customers. Online advertising is used to target specific demographics, such as age, gender, location, and interests. This allows businesses to tailor their messaging to the right audience and maximize their return on investment.

Online advertising is an invaluable tool for businesses looking to grow and succeed. It is cost-effective, allows businesses to reach a wider audience, and can be tailored to specific demographics. It helps businesses track and measure the success of their campaigns, allowing them to make informed decisions about their marketing strategies.

Social Media Marketing

Social media marketing is the process of using social media platforms to promote and market a product or service. It is a powerful tool for businesses of all sizes to reach their target audience, build relationships, and increase brand awareness.

Social media marketing has a significant impact on business growth. It helps businesses to reach a wider audience, build relationships with potential customers, and increase brand awareness. It also helps businesses to generate leads, increase website traffic, and boost sales.

Social media marketing helps businesses to build relationships with their target audience. This is done by engaging with customers, responding to their questions and comments, and providing helpful content. This helps to build trust and loyalty, which leads to increased sales.

Social media marketing also helps businesses to increase their visibility. By posting regularly on social media, businesses ensure that their content is seen by a wider audience. This help to increase brand awareness and reach potential customers who may not have otherwise been aware of the business.

Social media marketing has a significant impact on business growth. It helps businesses to reach a wider audience, build relationships with potential customers, and increase brand awareness. It also helps businesses to generate leads, increase website traffic, and boost sales.

Points to consider for Social Media Marketing

- **Develop a social media strategy**: Establish goals and objectives, determine target audiences, and create a content plan.

- **Identify the right social media channels**: Choose the channels that best fit your business and target audience.

- **Create engaging content**: Post content that is interesting, relevant, and shareable.

- **Monitor conversations**: Monitor conversations and respond to comments, questions, and complaints.

- **Engage with influencers**: Identify and engage with influencers in your industry to help spread your message.

- **Analyze data**: Track and analyze data to measure the success of your social media campaigns.

- **Use visuals**: Use visuals such as images, videos, and infographics to make your content more engaging.

- **Leverage automation**: Automate certain tasks to save time and resources.

- **Advertise**: Use social media advertising to reach a larger audience and drive more traffic to your website.

- **Offer incentives**: Offer incentives such as discounts and giveaways to encourage people to follow and engage with your brand

- **Promote user-generated content**: Encourage customers to share their experiences with your brand and promote their content.

- **Utilize social media tools**: Use social media tools to help you manage and measure your campaigns.

- **Stay up-to-date**: Stay up-to-date with the latest trends and changes in the social media landscape.

- **Measure ROI**: Measure the return on investment (ROI) of your social media campaigns.

- **Monitor competitors**: Monitor your competitors' social media activity to stay ahead

Networking

Networking is a critical component of business growth. It involves the development of relationships with other people and organizations in order to gain access to resources, contacts, and opportunities that help a business grow. Networking is used to build relationships, increase visibility, and generate leads. It can also be used to gain access to new markets, expand the customer base, and develop strategic partnerships.

The impact of networking on business growth is significant. Networking help businesses identify potential customers, partners, and suppliers. It also helps to create a positive reputation and build trust. Networking also helps to create opportunities for collaboration and joint ventures. By leveraging the networks of others, businesses can gain access to new resources, contacts, and ideas that help your company to grow.

Networking also helps to build relationships with key stakeholders, such as investors, customers, and suppliers. By developing your relationships with these stakeholders, businesses gain access to valuable resources and contacts that help your company to grow. Networking help to create a positive reputation for the business, which leads to more customers and increased   sales.

Networking helps to create a sense of community and collaboration. By connecting with other businesses and individuals, businesses gain access to new ideas, resources, and contacts. Networking helps to create a sense of camaraderie and support, which helps to foster innovation and creativity.

Trade Shows

A trade show is an event where companies in a particular industry come together to showcase their products and services to potential buyers. Trade shows provide an opportunity for businesses to network, build relationships, and increase their visibility in the market. They also allow companies to demonstrate their products and services to a large number of potential buyers in one place.

Trade shows have a significant impact on business growth. They provide an opportunity for businesses to gain exposure and build relationships with potential customers. Trade shows also allow businesses to demonstrate their products and services to a large number of potential buyers in one place. This help to increase sales and generate leads.

Trade shows also provide an opportunity for businesses to network with other industry professionals. This help to build relationships and collaborations that lead to increased business growth. Trade shows provide businesses with valuable feedback from potential customers. This feedback is used to improve products and services, as well as to develop new products and services.

Trade shows are a way for businesses to gain exposure, build relationships, and increase their visibility in the market. They also provide businesses with valuable insights into the latest trends and developments in their industry, as well as valuable feedback from potential customers. All of these factors help to drive business growth.

Cold Calling

Cold calling is a direct sales technique in which a salesperson contacts potential customers by telephone in an effort to solicit sales. It is a form of direct marketing and is often used to generate leads, build relationships, and increase sales. Cold calling is a difficult and often tedious task, but it is an effective way to reach potential customers and generate sales.

Cold calling is an effective way to reach out to potential customers and build relationships. It allows salespeople to introduce their products and services to a wider audience and is used to generate leads and close sales. Cold calling also allows salespeople to build relationships with potential customers and build trust.

However, cold calling can be a difficult and time-consuming process. It requires salespeople to have a good understanding of their product or service and the ability to effectively communicate their message. It also requires salespeople to be persistent and have the   ability   to   handle   rejection.

The impact of cold calling on business growth depends on how it is used. If used correctly, cold calling is an effective way to reach potential customers and generate sales. However, if used incorrectly, it is a waste of time and resources.

Email Marketing

Email marketing is a powerful tool for businesses to reach their target customers and promote their products and services. It is an effective way to build relationships with customers, increase brand awareness, and drive sales. Email marketing has been around for decades, but it has become increasingly popular in recent years due to the rise of digital marketing and the availability of powerful tools to automate   and   personalize   campaigns.

Email marketing is a cost-effective way to reach customers and prospects. It is also highly targeted, allowing businesses to send messages to the right people at the right time. Email marketing is used to nurture leads, build relationships, and drive sales. It can also be used to promote new products, announce special offers, and provide customer service.

The impact of email marketing on business growth is significant. Studies have shown that email marketing has a higher return on investment (ROI) than other marketing channels, such as search engine optimization (SEO) and social media. Email marketing helps businesses increase their revenue by driving more sales and leads. It also helps businesses build relationships with customers, increase brand awareness, and drive customer loyalty.

Email marketing is a powerful tool for businesses of all sizes. It is an effective way to reach customers, build relationships, and drive sales. By leveraging the power of email marketing, businesses increase their revenue and grow their business.

Affiliate Marketing

Affiliate marketing is a type of performance-based marketing in which a business rewards one or more affiliates for each visitor or customer brought by the affiliate's own marketing efforts. It is a modern variation of the practice of paying finder's fees for the introduction of new clients to a business.

Affiliate marketing has become a popular way for businesses to expand their reach and increase their sales. It is an effective way to drive traffic to a website, generate leads, and increase sales. It is also a cost-effective way to increase brand awareness and build relationships with potential customers.

The impact of affiliate marketing on business growth is significant. It helps businesses reach new customers, increase their sales, and build relationships with their customers. It also helps businesses to increase their visibility and reach a larger audience. It helps businesses to increase their profits by reducing their marketing costs.

Affiliate marketing is a bonding for businesses to increase their sales and reach a larger audience.

Referral Programs

A referral program is a marketing strategy used by businesses to encourage customers to refer new customers to the business. Referral programs are usually structured so that customers receive a reward for referring new customers. This reward may be in the form of a discount, cash, or other incentives.

The impact of referral programs on business growth is significant. Referral programs help businesses increase their customer base, increase sales, and improve customer loyalty. Referral programs also help businesses build relationships with their customers, as customers are more likely to refer a business to their friends and family if they have had a positive experience with the business.

Referral programs also help businesses increase their visibility, as customers who refer a business to their friends and family are likely to share their experiences on social media. This help businesses reach a wider audience and increase their brand awareness.

Referral programs help businesses build trust with their customers, as customers are more likely to trust a business that has been recommended to them by someone they know. This trust can lead to increased customer loyalty, which results in increased sales and business growth.

Referral programs have a positive impact on business growth. By offering rewards to customers for referring new customers, businesses increase their customer base, increase sales, and improve customer loyalty. Referral programs help businesses increase their visibility, build relationships with their customers, and build trust. All of these factors contribute to increased business growth.

Public Relations

Public relations (PR) is the practice of managing the spread of information between an individual or an organization and the public. It is an important part of any business's marketing strategy, as it helps to create a positive public image and build relationships with stakeholders.

The primary goal of public relations is to shape and maintain a positive public image for a company or individual. This is done by creating and maintaining relationships with the media, as well as creating and distributing content that is favorable to the company or individual. PR professionals also work to build relationships with key stakeholders, such as customers, investors, and government officials.

Public relations have a major impact on a business's growth. A positive public image help to attract new customers, investors, and partners. It also helps to build trust with existing customers and stakeholders, which can lead to increased sales and loyalty. A good public image help to protect a company from negative publicity, which has a major impact on a company's reputation.

Public relations also help to increase a company's visibility and reach. PR professionals help to create content that is shared on social media and other platforms, which helps to spread awareness of a company's products and services. PR professionals help to create relationships with influencers, which help to increase a company's reach and visibility.

Public relation is an important part of any business's marketing strategy. It helps to create a positive public image, build relationships with stakeholders, and increase a company's visibility and reach. All of these factors have a major impact on a business's

Content Marketing

Content marketing is a strategic marketing approach focused on creating and distributing valuable, relevant, and consistent content to attract and retain a clearly defined audience — and, ultimately, to drive profitable customer action.

Content marketing is used by businesses of all sizes and in all industries to build brand awareness, generate leads, and increase sales. It is an effective way to reach and engage customers, as well as to create meaningful relationships with them.

Content marketing is an important part of any business's overall marketing strategy. It helps to create a positive customer experience, build trust, and establish a brand's credibility. It also allows businesses to reach a wider audience and increase their   visibility.

Content marketing has a positive impact on business growth by helping to generate leads, increase website traffic, and boost sales. It also helps to build brand loyalty and trust, which leads to repeat customers and increased customer lifetime value.

Content marketing also helps to improve search engine rankings, as content that is relevant and of high-quality help to boost a website's ranking in search engine results. This leads to increased website traffic and more potential customers.

Content marketing also helps to build relationships with customers, as it allows businesses to provide valuable information that helps to educate and inform customers. This help to build trust and loyalty, which leads to increased sales and customer loyalty.

Content marketing is a powerful tool for businesses of all sizes and in all industries. It helps to build brand awareness, generate leads, and increase sales. It also helps to improve search engine rankings, build relationships with customers, and increase customer loyalty.

Influencer Marketing

Influencer marketing is a type of marketing that focuses on using key leaders to drive your brand's message to the larger market. Rather than marketing directly to a large group of consumers, you instead inspire/influence/hire influencers to get out the word for you. Influencers can be anyone from celebrities to everyday people with a large social media following.

The impact of influencer marketing on business growth is significant. It has been found to be one of the most effective forms of marketing, with an average return on investment of $6.50 for every dollar spent. This is because influencers have the ability to reach a large audience quickly, and their endorsement of a product or service carries more weight than traditional advertising.

In addition, influencer marketing helps build brand awareness and trust. Influencers have the ability to create a personal connection with their followers, which helps build loyalty and trust in a brand. This led to increased sales and customer retention.

Influencer marketing helps businesses reach new audiences. By partnering with influencers, businesses can tap into new markets and demographics that may not have been exposed to their products or services before. This help businesses expand their reach and increase their customer base.

Influencer marketing is an effective and powerful tool for businesses looking to grow their brand and increase their sales. It helps build trust and loyalty, reach new audiences, and generate a high return on investment.

Search Engine Optimization

Search Engine Optimization (SEO) is the process of optimizing a website or web page to increase its visibility in search engine results. SEO helps to ensure that a website is accessible to a search engine and improves the chances that the website will be found by the search engine. SEO is an important part of any business's online presence, as it helps to drive organic traffic to the website and leads to increased sales and brand awareness.

SEO is a long-term strategy that involves optimizing a website for specific keywords and phrases that are relevant to the business's products or services. SEO involves optimizing the website's content, structure, and code to make it more attractive to search engines. SEO also involves building links from other websites to the website, as well as optimizing the website's social media presence.

The impact of SEO on business growth is significant. SEO helps to increase organic traffic to a website, which leads to increased sales and brand awareness. SEO also helps to improve the website's visibility in search engine results, which leads to more people finding the website and engaging with the business. SEO also helps to improve the website's usability, which leads to increased customer satisfaction and loyalty.

SEO is an important part of any business's online presence and has a significant impact on business growth. SEO helps to increase organic traffic to the website, improve the website's visibility in search engine results, and improve the website's usability. All of these factors lead to increased sales and brand awareness, which help to drive business growth.

Mobile Advertising

Mobile advertising is a form of digital marketing that uses mobile devices to reach potential customers. It is a rapidly growing form of advertising that be used to target customers in a variety of ways, including location-based targeting, contextual targeting, and demographic targeting. Mobile advertising is used to promote products, services, and events, as well as to drive traffic to websites and increase brand awareness.

The impact of mobile advertising on business growth is significant. According to a study, mobile advertising spending is expected to reach $257.5 billion by 2025, up from $69.9 billion in 2016. This growth is driven by the increasing number of people using mobile devices to access the internet, as well as the increasing number of people using mobile devices to make purchases.

Mobile advertising is used to reach potential customers in a variety of ways. For example, location-based targeting can be used to target customers in a specific geographic area. Contextual targeting is used to target customers based on their interests or behavior. Demographic targeting is used to target customers based on their age, gender, or other demographic characteristics.

Mobile advertising also is used to increase brand awareness. By leveraging the power of mobile devices, businesses reach potential customers in a more personal and engaging way. Mobile advertising also is used to drive traffic to websites, increase app downloads, and generate leads.

In addition to increasing brand awareness and driving traffic, mobile advertising also is used to increase sales. By targeting customers with relevant ads, businesses increase their chances of making a sale. Mobile advertising also is used to increase customer loyalty by engaging customers with personalized messages and offers.

Print Advertising

Print advertising is a form of advertising that uses physically printed media, such as magazines, newspapers, and direct mail, to reach a targeted audience. It is one of the oldest forms of advertising, with a long history of success. Print advertising is an effective way to reach a large audience and help businesses grow and expand their reach.

Print advertising is used to target a specific audience, such as a certain age group or geographic area. It also is used to reach a wide audience, such as a national or global market. Print advertising is used to promote a product or service, create brand awareness, and increase sales. It also is used to build relationships with customers, increase customer loyalty, and create a positive brand image.

Print advertising is used in a variety of ways to reach a targeted audience. It is used to create direct mail campaigns, place advertisements in newspapers and magazines, and distribute flyers. It is also be used to create billboards, posters, and other forms of outdoor advertising.

Print advertising is a cost-effective way to reach a large audience and help businesses grow and expand their reach.

Radio Advertising

Radio advertising is a powerful tool for businesses of all sizes. It is an effective way to reach a large audience, and it is used to target specific demographics. Radio advertising is used to create brand awareness, increase sales, and drive customer loyalty.

Radio advertising is a cost-effective way to reach a large audience. It is relatively inexpensive compared to other forms of advertising, such as television or print. Radio advertising can also be tailored to specific demographics, allowing businesses to target their message to the right people.

Radio advertising is used to create brand awareness. It is used to introduce a new product or service to the public, or to remind people of an existing product or service. Radio advertising can also be used to increase sales. It is used to promote a sale or special offer, or to encourage people to purchase a product or service.

Radio advertising can also be used to drive customer loyalty. By creating a consistent message, businesses can build a relationship with their customers. This can lead to repeat customers and increased sales.

Radio advertising can also be used to reach a wide variety of audiences. It is used to target specific age groups, genders, or geographic areas. This allows businesses to tailor their message to the right people.

Radio advertising can have a positive impact on business growth. It is used to create brand awareness, increase sales, and drive customer loyalty. It is a cost-effective way to reach a large audience, and it can be tailored to specific demographics. Radio advertising is an effective tool for businesses of all sizes.

Television Advertising

Television advertising is one of the most powerful and effective forms of advertising available to businesses today. It has the potential to reach a large audience, generate brand awareness, and increase sales. Television advertising is used to target specific audiences, create an emotional connection with viewers, and build brand loyalty.

The impact of television advertising on business growth is significant. Studies have shown that television advertising can increase brand awareness and recognition, create an emotional connection with viewers, and increase sales. It can also help to build brand loyalty, as viewers become familiar with the brand and its products.

Television advertising can also be used to target specific audiences. Companies can use demographic data to determine which viewers are most likely to be interested in their products or services. This allows them to tailor their advertising to those viewers, increasing the likelihood that they will respond to the ad.

Companies can use music, visuals, and storytelling to create an emotional response in viewers. This can help to create an emotional bond between the viewer and the brand, increasing the likelihood that they will remember the brand and purchase its products or services.

Television advertising is used to build brand loyalty. Companies can use television advertising to create an ongoing relationship with viewers. This can include offering discounts or promotions to viewers who watch the ad or creating a series of ads that tell a story about the brand. This can help to create a sense of loyalty among viewers, increasing the likelihood that they will continue to purchase the brand's products   or   services.

In conclusion, television advertising can have a significant impact on business growth. It is used to target specific audiences

Points to consider for Television Advertising.

- **Target Audience**: Identify the target audience for the television ad and tailor the message to meet their needs.

- **Budget**: Determine a realistic budget for the television ad and make sure it fits within the overall marketing budget.

- **Timing**: Choose the best time to air the ad to ensure maximum reach and impact.

- **Creative**: Develop a creative concept for the ad that will capture the attention of the target audience.

- **Script**: Write a script that conveys the message clearly and concisely.

- **Production**: Hire a professional production company to produce the ad.

- **Voiceover**: Select a voiceover artist who will bring the script to life.

- **Music**: Choose music that will enhance the ad and create the desired mood.

- **Visuals**: Select visuals that will help to communicate the message.

- **Placement**: Decide where the ad will be placed in the television schedule.

- **Duration**: Determine the length of the ad and make sure it fits within the allotted time.

- **Frequency**: Decide how often the ad should be aired to maximize its impact.

- **Tracking**: Implement a tracking system to measure the success of the ad.

- **Evaluation**: Analyze the results of the ad and make adjustments as needed.

- **ROI**: Calculate the return on investment of the ad to determine its effectiveness.

- **Branding**: Utilize the ad to increase brand awareness and recognition.

- **Promotions**: Use the ad to promote special offers and discounts.

Trade Publications

Trade publications, also known as trade journals, are magazines or newspapers that focus on a specific industry or sector, such as finance, technology, or healthcare. They provide news, analysis, and opinions about the industry, as well as information about new products and services. Trade publications are often used by businesses to stay up to date on industry trends and to gain insights into their competitors.

Trade publications can have a significant impact on business growth. They provide businesses with valuable information about the industry, such as market trends, new products and services, and emerging technologies. This information can help businesses make informed decisions about their strategies and operations. Trade publications can help businesses identify potential partners, customers, and suppliers.

Trade publications can also be used to promote a business's products and services. By advertising in trade publications, businesses can reach their target audience and increase their visibility. Businesses can use trade publications to build relationships with industry leaders and influencers. This can help businesses establish credibility and gain access to new markets.

Trade publications can help businesses stay ahead of the competition. By reading trade publications, businesses can stay up to date on industry trends and gain insights into their competitors' strategies. This can help businesses stay one step ahead of the competition and position themselves for success.

Outdoor Advertising

Outdoor advertising is a form of advertising that uses physical structures to promote products, services, and brands. It includes billboards, signs, posters, banners, and other forms of visual communication. Outdoor advertising is one of the oldest forms of advertising, and it is still one of the most effective ways to reach a large audience.

Outdoor advertising has the potential to reach a large number of people in a short amount of time. It is often used to create brand awareness and to drive sales. It can also be used to create a sense of urgency and to encourage people to take action. Outdoor advertising can be used to target specific audiences, such as those in a certain geographic area or those with specific interests.

Outdoor advertising is also cost-effective. It is often cheaper than other forms of advertising, such as television and radio. It is also more flexible, as it can be changed quickly and easily.

Outdoor advertising can have a positive impact on business growth.

Points to be considered for Outdoor advertising.

- **Location**: Selecting the right location for outdoor advertising is critical for its success. Choose locations with high foot traffic and visibility.

- **Timing**: Timing is key when it comes to outdoor advertising. Consider when people are most likely to see the ad and plan accordingly.

- **Design**: Make sure your outdoor advertising is eye-catching and memorable. Use bright colors, bold fonts, and an attractive design.

- **Target Audience**: Know your target audience and tailor your outdoor advertising to them. Consider their age, gender, interests, and other demographic information.

- **Cost**: Outdoor advertising can be expensive, so make sure you have a budget in place. Consider your return on investment when deciding how much to spend.

- **Measurement**: Track your outdoor advertising campaigns to measure their effectiveness. Use metrics such as impressions, clicks, and conversions to determine if your campaigns are successful.

- **Variety**: Try different types of outdoor advertising to reach different audiences. Consider billboards, bus stops, and other forms of outdoor advertising.

- **Frequency**: Make sure your outdoor advertising is seen often. Consider running multiple campaigns in the same area to increase visibility.

- **Consistency**: Keep your outdoor advertising consistent with your other marketing efforts. Use the same branding, messaging, and visuals across all of your campaigns.

- **Social Media**: Leverage social media to increase the reach of your outdoor advertising. Use hashtags, links, and other tactics to drive people to your website or social media accounts.

- **Interactivity**: Make your outdoor advertising interactive by adding QR codes, augmented reality, or other interactive elements.

Point of Sale Advertising

Point of sale (POS) advertising is a type of marketing that is used to promote products and services at the point of sale. It is a form of in-store advertising that is used to increase sales and brand awareness. POS advertising is used to draw attention to products and services and to encourage customers to purchase them.

POS advertising can be used in a variety of ways, including displays, posters, banners, signs, and other materials. It can also be used in combination with other marketing techniques, such as coupons, discounts, and promotions.

POS advertising is an effective way to reach customers at the point of purchase. It is used to increase sales by reminding customers of the product or service, as well as to create brand awareness. It can also be used to inform customers of special offers and promotions.

POS advertising can have a positive impact on business growth. It can help to increase sales and brand awareness, as well as to create a positive impression of the business. It can also help to increase customer loyalty, as customers are more likely to return to a store if they have a positive experience.

POS advertising can be a cost-effective way to reach customers. It can be used to target specific customers, such as those who are likely to purchase a particular product or service. It can also be used to reach a wider audience, such as those who may not be aware of the product or service.

POS advertising is used to create a positive impression of the business. It is used to show customers that the business is professional and reliable. It can also be used to create a sense of urgency, as customers may be more likely to purchase a product or service if they feel.

CHAPTER TEN

Create the Budget and Financial Plan

Creating a budget and financial plan for a new business is an important step in the process of starting a business. It is essential to have a clear understanding of the financial resources available to the business and how they will be used.

Financial planning for a new business is an important step in ensuring the success of the business. It involves analyzing the current financial situation, setting financial goals, and developing strategies to reach those goals.

- **Analyzing the Current Financial Situation**: This involves looking at the current financial situation of the business, including cash flow, income, expenses, assets, liabilities, and net worth. This analysis will help you identify any potential problems and areas that need improvement.

- **Setting Financial Goals**: Once you have a clear understanding of the current financial situation, you set financial goals for the business. These goals should be realistic and achievable and should include short-term and long-term goals with the financial targets that need to be met.

- **Developing Strategies**: After setting financial goals, you need to develop strategies to reach those goals. This may include budgeting, investing, and debt management.

- **Monitoring Progress**: Once you have established your financial goals and strategies, you need to monitor progress to ensure that the goals are being met. This can be done by tracking income and expenses and comparing them to the goals.

- **Analyze the Market**: The next step is to analyze the market. What is the size of the market? Who are the competitors? What are the trends in the industry?

- **Estimate Start-up Costs**: Once the goals and market analysis have been completed, the next step is to estimate the start-up costs for the business. This includes the cost of equipment, supplies, inventory, and any other costs associated with getting the business up and running.

- **Estimate Operating Expenses**: After the start-up costs have been estimated, the next step is to estimate the operating expenses. This includes the cost of labor, rent, utilities, insurance, advertising, and other expenses associated with running the business.

- **Create a Budget**: Once the start-up costs and operating expenses have been estimated, the next step is to create a budget. This includes setting a budget for each expense category and creating a timeline for when the expenses will be incurred.

- **Create a Financial Plan**: The final step in creating a budget and financial plan for a new business is to create a financial plan. This includes creating a cash flow projection, setting up a system for tracking income and expenses

Financial planning for a new business is an important step in ensuring the success of the business. By analyzing the current financial situation, setting financial goals, developing strategies to reach those goals, and monitoring progress, you can ensure that your business is on the right track.

CHAPTER ELEVEN

Securing Funding and Capital

Securing funding and capital for a new business is a critical and often challenging process. It is important to understand the different sources of funding available and to develop a comprehensive strategy for obtaining the necessary capital.

The first step in securing funding and capital for a new business is to assess the current financial situation. This includes evaluating the current cash flow, the amount of debt, and the level of equity. It is important to understand the financial needs of the business and to develop a plan for how the money will be used.

Once the financial situation has been assessed, the next step is to identify potential sources of funding and capital. These sources may include traditional lenders such as banks, venture capitalists, angel investors, and government grants. It is important to research the different options available and to determine which ones are most suitable for the business.

Once the sources of funding and capital have been identified, the next step is to create a financial plan. This plan should include detailed information about the business costs, including the product costs and service costs offered, the target market availability, the competitive landscape, and the financial projections. This plan should also include a detailed description of the proposed use of the funds, and a timeline for when the funds will be used.

Once the financial plan has been created, the next step is to present the plan to potential investors. This may involve presenting the plan to banks, venture capitalists, angel investors, or government agencies. It is important to be prepared to answer any questions that may arise and to provide detailed information about the business and the proposed use of the funds.

Once the funding and capital have been secured, it is important to develop a plan for how the money will be utilized

Various means and ways of securing funding and capital
Crowdfunding

Crowdfunding is a way of raising money for a project or business venture by asking a large number of people to contribute a small amount of money. It is usually done through an online platform. Crowdfunding can help new businesses by providing them with access to capital that they may not have been able to access otherwise. It also allows them to test the market for your product or service and gauge the level of interest in it. It is used to build a community of supporters around the business, which is invaluable for marketing and promotion.

Angel Investors

Angel investors are individuals who provide capital to start-ups in exchange for equity. They typically invest their own money and are usually high-net-worth individuals. Angel investors provide much-needed capital to start-ups when traditional financing is not available. They also provide valuable advice and mentorship to you, helping you to develop and grow your businesses. Angel investors often have a vested interest in the success of the business and can provide invaluable guidance to help the business succeed.

Bank Loans

Bank loans are funds that are lent by a bank to a business or individual. They are typically used to finance large purchases or investments, such as buying a new building, buying equipment, or expanding a business. Bank loans are usually secured by collateral, such as a business's assets or a personal home.

Bank loans can be a good option for your businesses to get the capital needed to get started. By taking out a loan, you can purchase the equipment, supplies, and other resources you need to get your business up and running. Bank loans can be used to finance the expansion of an existing business, allowing it to grow and increase its profits.

Bank loans can help new businesses by providing them with access to capital that is used to purchase equipment, hire employees, and cover operating expenses. Bank loans can also provide businesses with the opportunity to build a credit history, which is beneficial for future financing. Bank loans can provide businesses with the flexibility to pay back the loan over a longer period of time, allowing you to focus on growing your business.

Venture Capital

Venture capitalists are investors who provide capital to start-up companies and small businesses that are deemed to have long-term growth potential. Venture capitalists can help new businesses by providing capital to help them grow, as well as offering advice and guidance on how to best use the funds. They can also help with networking and introductions to potential partners and customers.

Venture capitalists are investors who provide capital to businesses in exchange for equity. They are typically high-net-worth individuals, investment firms, or banks that specialize in providing capital to early-stage companies. Venture capitalists typically invest in companies that have the potential to grow quickly and generate high returns.

Venture capitalists can provide new businesses with the capital they need to get off the ground and grow. They can also provide valuable advice and mentorship to entrepreneurs, helping them to make the right decisions and navigate the complexities of the start-up world. Venture capitalists can also help new businesses to secure additional funding, such as from angel investors or other venture capital firms.

Venture capitalists typically look for companies that have a strong management team, a clear business plan, and a product or service that has the potential to scale quickly. They also look for companies that have the potential to generate high returns on their investments.

Venture capitalists can be a great source of funding and advice for new businesses. However, it is important to remember that venture capitalists are looking to make a return on their investments, so you should be prepared to give up a portion of your company in exchange for the capital you receive.

Small Business Grants

Small business grants are funds that are provided by government or private organizations to help new businesses get started. These grants can provide capital to cover start-up costs, purchase equipment, hire employees, and more. Grants can be used to cover a wide range of expenses, including marketing, research and development, and operational costs. Grants can also be used to help businesses expand or diversify their operations. Grants are an opportunity for new businesses to get the capital they need to get off the ground and become successful.

Small business grants help new businesses get off the ground. Grants can provide much-needed capital to help entrepreneurs launch their businesses and cover the costs of getting started. Grants can also be used to help businesses expand their operations, purchase new equipment, hire new employees, and more.

The first step in applying for a small business grant is to determine which grants are available. There are a variety of grants available, from Central and state grants to private grants from foundations and other organizations. It is important to research the different types of grants available and determine which ones are the best fit for your business.

Once you have identified the grants that are available, you will need to complete an application. The application process can vary depending on the grant, but typically requires a detailed business plan, financial statements, and other supporting documents. It is important to be thorough and accurate when completing the application in order to maximize your chances of being awarded the grant.

Once the application is submitted, the grant review process can take several weeks or months. During this time, the grant review board will review the application and make a decision on whether or not to award the grant. If the grant is awarded, the funds will be distributed to the business and used for the specified purpose.

Small business grants help to get a new business off the ground. They can provide the necessary capital to cover start-up costs, purchase new equipment, hire new employees, and more. It is important to research the different types of grants available and complete a thorough and accurate application in order to maximize your chances of being awarded the grant.

Family and Friends

Family and friends are a great source of support for new businesses. They can provide emotional and financial support, as well as practical advice and assistance. Here are some of the ways that family and friends can help new businesses:

- **Financial Support**: Family and friends can provide financial support to new businesses, either through direct investments or loans. This is good support to get the business off the ground, as it can provide the necessary capital to get started.

- **Emotional and Moral Support**: Starting a business is a stressful and challenging process. Having family and friends to lean on can provide the emotional support needed to get through tough times. Family and friends can provide the support needed to help the business owner stay motivated and focused on the task at hand.

- **Practical Advice**: Family and friends can provide valuable advice and guidance on how to start and run a business. They may have experience in the industry or know someone who does and can provide valuable insight into the process.

- **Networking**: Family and friends can help to expand the business's network by introducing them to potential customers, suppliers, and partners. This will help to get the business off the ground and increase its reach.

- **Promotion**: Family and friends can help to promote the business by spreading the word about it to their own network. This is a good method to get the business noticed and increase its customer base.

- **Seed Money**: Family and friends can provide the initial capital needed to get a business off the ground. This is done through a loan or an investment in exchange for equity in the business.

- **Mentorship**: Family and friends can provide invaluable advice and guidance to help the business owner make informed decisions.

- **Promotion**: Family and friends can help spread the word about the business by talking it up to their own contacts and social media followers.

- **Free Services**: Family and friends can offer their services for free or at a discounted rate to help the business get started. This could include accounting, legal, marketing, or web design services.

- **Crowdfunding**: Family and friends can help the business owner raise money through crowdfunding platforms.

- **Angel Investors**: Family and friends can introduce the business to angel investors who can provide larger amounts of capital in exchange for equity in the business.

Family and friends can be great sources of support for new businesses. They can provide financial, emotional, and practical support, as well as help to expand the business's network and promote it to their own networks.

Business Credit Cards

Business credit cards are a type of credit card specifically designed to meet the needs of businesses. They are designed to help businesses manage their cash flow, make purchases, and track expenses. Business credit cards offer a variety of benefits, including rewards, cash back, and other incentives.

Business credit cards can help businesses in a variety of ways. They can help businesses manage their cash flow by providing access to funds when needed. Businesses can use the cards to make purchases, pay for services, and cover other expenses. Business credit cards also help businesses track expenses, making it easier to manage finances.

Business credit cards can also help businesses build their credit. Businesses can use the cards to establish a credit history and build a good credit score. This is beneficial when applying for loans or other financings.

Business credit cards can also provide businesses with rewards and cash back. Many business credit cards offer rewards programs, such as points or cash back, which are used to purchase items or services. This can help businesses save money and increase their bottom line.

Business credit cards can also help businesses with start-up costs. Many business credit cards offer low introductory rates and other incentives, such as no annual fees, that can help businesses get started. This can help businesses save money and reduce their start-up costs.

Business credit cards can be a great tool for businesses of all sizes. They can help businesses manage their cash flow, make purchases, and track expenses. They can also help businesses build their credit and save money with rewards and cash back. Business credit cards can be generally good to help businesses get started and grow.

Business Incubators

A business incubator is a program designed to help new and start-up companies develop by providing services such as management training, access to financing, and office space. Business incubators are typically sponsored by universities, economic development organizations, or government agencies. The goal of a business incubator is to help entrepreneurs launch and grow their businesses, and to create jobs and economic development in the local community.

Business incubators provide a range of services to help entrepreneurs launch and grow their businesses. These services may include:

- **Management training**: Business incubators provide training on topics such as business planning, marketing, accounting, and legal issues.

- **Access to financing**: Business incubators can help entrepreneurs access financing from venture capitalists, angel investors, and other sources.

- **Office space**: Business incubators provide office space for entrepreneurs to use while they are launching and growing their businesses.

- **Mentoring**: Business incubators provide mentoring and advice from experienced entrepreneurs and business professionals.

- **Networking**: Business incubators can help entrepreneurs network with other entrepreneurs, investors, and potential customers.

- **Technology**: Business incubators can provide access to the latest technology and resources to help entrepreneurs launch and grow their businesses.

Business incubators can be a great resource for entrepreneurs who are launching and growing their businesses. They provide access to resources, training, and mentoring that can help entrepreneurs succeed. Business incubators can help create jobs and economic development in the local community.

Business Competitions

Business competitions are events that challenge entrepreneurs to develop innovative and creative solutions to real-world business problems. Competitions are designed to encourage entrepreneurs to think outside the box, come up with new ideas, and develop their business skills.

Business competitions provide a platform for entrepreneurs to showcase their skills, network with potential investors, and gain valuable feedback from experts. Competitions also provide a great opportunity for entrepreneurs to gain exposure and recognition for their business ideas.

Business competitions can help start-ups in a variety of ways. First, they provide a platform for entrepreneurs to practice their skills and develop their business ideas. Competitions also provide a great opportunity for entrepreneurs to network with potential investors and gain valuable feedback from experts.

In addition, business competitions can provide start-ups with access to funding and resources. Many competitions offer prizes such as cash, mentorship, and access to incubators and accelerators. These resources are invaluable for start-ups looking to get their business off the ground.

Business competitions can help start-ups gain recognition and exposure. Winning a competition is very nice to get your business noticed and attract potential investors. Competitions can also provide a great platform for entrepreneurs to showcase their skills and ideas to a wider audience.

Business competitions help start-ups to gain exposure, resources, and recognition. Competitions can provide entrepreneurs with the opportunity to practice their skills, network with potential investors, and gain valuable feedback from experts. Ultimately, business competitions are great for start-ups to get their business off the ground.

Microloans

Microloans are small loans, usually ranging from $500 to $50,000, that is designed to help entrepreneurs and small business owners access capital to start or expand their businesses. These loans are typically provided by non-profit organizations, government programs, or specialized microlenders.

Microloans are beneficial for entrepreneurs and small business owners because they provide access to capital that may not be available through traditional bank loans. Microloans are often easier to obtain than traditional loans, and they often have more flexible repayment terms. Microloans can provide access to capital to entrepreneurs who may not have the credit score or collateral needed to secure a traditional loan.

Microloans can be used for a variety of purposes, including purchasing equipment, hiring employees, launching a marketing campaign, or expanding into new markets. These loans can also be used to cover the costs of starting a business, such as licensing fees, legal fees, and business plan development.

Microloans can be a good source for entrepreneurs and small business owners to access capital to start or expand their businesses. These loans can provide access to capital that may not be available through traditional bank loans, and they often have more flexible repayment terms. Microloans can provide access to capital to entrepreneurs who may not have the credit score or collateral needed to secure a traditional loan.

Personal Savings

Personal savings are a key component of any business development and start-up. Having a healthy savings account can help entrepreneurs to cover the costs of starting a business, as well as provide a cushion in case of unexpected expenses. Savings can also be used to invest in the business, allowing entrepreneurs to take advantage of opportunities that may arise.

The first step in using personal savings to develop a business is to create a budget. This budget should include all of the necessary expenses associated with starting the business, such as rent, utilities, and supplies. Once the budget is created, the entrepreneur should set aside a portion of their income each month to put into savings. This will help to ensure that there is enough money available to cover the costs of starting the business.

Once the business is up and running, the entrepreneur should continue to save a portion of their income. This money is used to invest in the business, such as purchasing new equipment or hiring additional staff. It can also be used to cover unexpected expenses, such as repairs or unexpected costs.

Having a healthy savings account can also provide entrepreneurs with access to capital. This capital is used to expand the business, allowing the entrepreneur to take advantage of new opportunities. It can also be used as collateral for loans, allowing the entrepreneur to access additional funds if needed.

Having a healthy savings account can provide entrepreneurs with peace of mind. Knowing that there is money set aside for unexpected expenses can help to reduce stress and allow entrepreneurs to focus on growing their businesses.

Personal savings are an essential part of your business development and start-up. By creating a budget and setting aside a portion of your income each month, you can ensure that you have sufficient liquidity for your business to kick start.

Government Grants

Government grants are a form of financial assistance provided by the government to help businesses develop. Grants are typically awarded to businesses that demonstrate a need for the funds and a commitment to using them for the intended purpose.

Government grants are used for a variety of purposes, including research and development, capital investments, marketing, and training. Grants can also be used to help businesses expand into new markets, hire additional staff, or purchase new equipment.

Government grants are typically awarded through a competitive process. Businesses must submit an application that outlines their project, the amount of funding requested, and how the funds will be used. Applications are then reviewed by a panel of experts who evaluate the project's potential for success.

Government grants can provide businesses with the financial resources they need to get off the ground and grow. Grants can help businesses cover the cost of research and development, capital investments, and marketing. Grants can also help businesses expand into new markets and hire additional staff.

Government grants are too good for businesses to get the funding they need to succeed. However, businesses must be aware of the application process and the potential risks associated with accepting government funds. Businesses should also be aware of the reporting requirements associated with government grants, as failure to comply can result in the funds being revoked.

Business Angels

Business angels are private investors who provide capital to start-up businesses in exchange for equity or convertible debt. They are typically wealthy individuals who are looking for higher returns than what they can get from traditional investments. Business angels are often entrepreneurs themselves and have experience in the industry they are investing in.

Business angels provide capital to start-up businesses in exchange for equity or convertible debt. This means that the business angel will own a portion of the company and will be entitled to a portion of the profits. The business angel may also receive a return on their investment if the company is successful.

Business angels provide more than just capital. They can also provide advice and mentorship to the entrepreneurs they invest in. They often have experience in the industry they are investing in and can provide valuable insights and guidance. They can also provide valuable connections to potential customers, suppliers, and other investors.

Business angels can provide start-ups with the capital they need to get off the ground. This is especially helpful for start-ups that are unable to secure traditional financing. Business angels can also provide valuable advice and mentorship that can help entrepreneurs succeed.

In conclusion, business angels can be a valuable source of capital and advice for start-ups. They can provide the capital needed to get a business off the ground and can also provide valuable advice and mentorship. Business angels are a great resource for entrepreneurs looking to start a business.

Online Lenders

Online lenders are a great option for businesses looking to develop and grow. They offer a variety of services and products that can help businesses of all sizes and stages of development. From start-ups to established businesses, online lenders can provide capital, advice, and support.

One of the main advantages of online lenders is their ability to provide quick access to capital. Many online lenders offer loans with quick approval and funding times, which is a great help for businesses that need money quickly. Online lenders also often offer more flexible repayment terms than traditional lenders, which can make it easier for businesses to manage their cash flow.

Online lenders also provide a variety of services and products that can help businesses grow and develop. For example, some online lenders offer business credit cards, which can be handy to build business credit and accessing additional capital. Other online lenders offer merchant cash advances, which are used to cover short-term expenses or to purchase inventory.

Online lenders can also provide valuable advice and support to businesses. Many online lenders have teams of experts who can provide guidance on a variety of topics, such as marketing, accounting, and finance. This is a great resource for businesses that are just starting out or need help navigating the complexities of running a business.

The online lender is a great resource for businesses looking to develop and grow. They offer quick access to capital, flexible repayment terms, and a variety of services and products that can help businesses succeed. With the right online lender, businesses can access the resources they need to succeed.

Peer-to-Peer Lending

Peer-to-peer (P2P) lending is a form of financing that allows individuals and businesses to borrow and lend money without the use of a traditional financial institution. It is an online platform that connects borrowers and lenders directly, allowing them to negotiate terms and interest rates. P2P lending has become increasingly popular in recent years, as it offers a more efficient, cost-effective, and transparent alternative to traditional financing.

For businesses, P2P lending is an attractive option for financing. It can provide access to capital quickly and with fewer restrictions than traditional lenders. Borrowers can often get funding in as little as a few days, and the process is typically much simpler than with a bank loan. P2P lenders also typically have lower interest rates and more flexible repayment terms than banks.

For start-ups, P2P lending is a great support to get the capital they need to get their business off the ground. Start-ups often have difficulty accessing traditional financing, as they lack the credit history and collateral that banks typically require. P2P lenders are more willing to take on riskier borrowers, and they can provide the capital start-ups need to get their businesses up and running.

P2P lending can also be valuable for businesses to diversify their financing sources. By using P2P lenders, businesses can access capital from a variety of sources, which can help reduce their overall risk. P2P lenders often offer more flexible repayment terms than traditional lenders, which can help businesses manage their cash flow more effectively.

Business Lines of Credit

A business line of credit is a type of loan that allows businesses to borrow money up to a certain limit. The money is used for any purpose, such as purchasing inventory, paying for operating expenses, or financing a new project. Unlike a traditional loan, a line of credit does not require the borrower to pay back the entire loan amount at once. Instead, the borrower can draw on the line of credit as needed and only pay interest on the amount borrowed.

Business lines of credit really help businesses to access the capital they need to grow and develop. They provide businesses with flexibility and access to funds when they need them, without having to take out a large loan or wait for an investor. This is especially helpful for start-ups, who often have limited access to capital.

Business lines of credit are used to cover a variety of expenses, including purchasing inventory, paying for operating expenses, or financing a new project. They can also be used to cover unexpected costs, such as repairs or emergency expenses. This flexibility makes them a great option for businesses that need to be able to access funds quickly.

Business lines of credit also provide businesses with

the ability to manage their cash flow more effectively. By having access to funds when needed, businesses can avoid having to take out large loans or wait for investors. This can help businesses manage their expenses more efficiently and help them stay on top of their cash flow.

Business lines of credit can help businesses build their credit score. By making regular payments on the line of credit, businesses can demonstrate their ability to manage debt responsibly and build their credit score. This is beneficial for businesses looking to secure additional financing in the future.

Equipment Financing

Equipment financing is a type of loan that allows businesses to purchase the equipment they need to operate and grow. It is a form of asset-based lending, which means that the loan is secured by the equipment being purchased. Equipment financing can be used to purchase a variety of items, including vehicles, computers, manufacturing equipment, and more.

Equipment financing is a great option for businesses that need to purchase equipment but don't have the cash on hand to do so. It can also be a great option for start-ups, as it allows them to acquire the equipment, they need to get their business up and running without having to use their own capital.

Equipment financing can help businesses in a number of ways. First, it allows businesses to acquire the equipment they need without having to use their own capital. This is especially beneficial for start-ups, as it allows them to get their business up and running without having to use their own resources.

Second, equipment financing can help businesses save money. Because the loan is secured by the equipment being purchased, the interest rate is typically lower than other types of financing. This can help businesses save money in the long run.

Third, equipment financing can help businesses save time. By financing the equipment they need, businesses can avoid the lengthy process of searching for and negotiating with vendors. This can help businesses save time and get the equipment they need quickly.

Equipment financing can help businesses maintain their cash flow. By financing the equipment they need, businesses can avoid having to use their own capital to purchase the equipment. This can help businesses maintain their cash flow and ensure that they have the funds they need to operate and grow.

Factoring

Factoring is a type of financing that helps businesses to access cash quickly and easily. It is a financial transaction in which a business sells its accounts receivable (invoices) to a third party (called a factor) at a discount. The factor then collects the payments from the customers and pays the business the discounted amount. Factoring is a nice way for businesses to access cash quickly and easily, and it can help them to grow and develop.

Factoring can be especially beneficial for small businesses and start-ups. These businesses often have limited access to traditional financing options such as bank loans, and factoring can provide them with the cash they need to grow and develop. Factoring can also help start-ups to manage their cash flow more effectively, as they can access cash quickly and easily without having to wait for customers to pay their invoices. This can help them to cover their short-term expenses and invest in new opportunities.

Factoring can also help businesses to reduce their risk. By selling their invoices to a factor, businesses can reduce their exposure to bad debt and credit risk. The factor will assume the risk of non-payment, meaning that businesses don't have to worry about customers not paying their invoices. This can help businesses to manage their finances more effectively and reduce their risk.

Factoring is a quick way for businesses to access cash quickly and easily, and it can be especially beneficial for small businesses and start-ups. It can help them to manage their cash flow more effectively, reduce their risk, and invest in new opportunities.

Initial Public Offering (IPO)

An Initial Public Offering (IPO) is the process by which a private company can become a publicly traded company by offering its shares to the public.

IPOs are a way for a company to raise capital and increase its visibility in the market. Through an IPO, a company can also increase its liquidity and attract more investors.

IPOs are a great business opportunity to set up for start-ups and small businesses to raise capital and expand their operations. By going public, a company can access a larger pool of potential investors, which can help it to raise more capital. Going public can also help a company to increase its visibility and credibility in the market, which can lead to more customers and business opportunities.

IPOs also provide a way for companies to reward their existing shareholders. By offering shares to the public, a company can provide its existing shareholders with the opportunity to sell their shares and realize a return on their investment. This is especially beneficial for early investors who have been with the company since its inception and have been waiting for the company to go public.

IPOs can also help a company attract and retain top talent. By going public, a company can offer its employees the opportunity to purchase shares in the company, which is a great incentive for them to stay with the company. Going public can also help a company to attract new talent, as it can demonstrate that the company is a viable and successful business.

A streamlined approach to IPOs can bring in a lot of visibility for start-ups and small businesses to raise capital and expand their operations. By going public, a company can access a larger pool of potential investors, increase its visibility and credibility in the market, reward its existing shareholders

Private Equity

Private equity (PE) is a form of alternative investment that involves the investment of capital into companies or funds that are not publicly traded on a stock exchange. Private equity firms typically invest in companies that are in need of capital for expansion, restructuring, or other purposes.

Private equity firms provide capital to companies in exchange for equity stakes in the company. This means that the private equity firm will own a portion of the company and will have a say in how the company is managed. Private equity firms also provide management expertise and advice to the companies they invest in.

Private equity firms can help businesses in a number of ways. They can provide capital for expansion, restructuring, or other purposes. They can also provide advice and guidance on how to best manage the company. Private equity firms can also help businesses develop strategies for growth and profitability.

Private equity firms can also help start-ups by providing capital to help them get off the ground. Start-ups often need capital to launch their business, but may not have access to traditional sources of financing. Private equity firms can provide the necessary capital to help start-ups get off the ground.

Private equity firms can also help start-ups by providing advice and guidance on how to best manage the business. Private equity firms can help start-ups develop strategies for growth and profitability. They can also provide advice on how to best structure the business, such as how to structure the ownership and management of the company.

Private equity firms can be a great source of capital and advice for businesses and start-ups. They can provide capital for expansion, restructuring, or other purposes. They can also provide advice and guidance on how to best manage the business.

Mergers and Acquisitions

Mergers and acquisitions (M&A) is a type of corporate restructuring that involves the combination of two or more companies into a single entity. This is done through either a merger, where one company is absorbed into another or an acquisition, where one company purchases another. M&A can be used to expand a company's market share, diversify its product offerings, or gain access to new technology or resources.

M&A is beneficial for both established companies and start-ups. For established companies, M&A can provide access to new markets, technologies, and resources, as well as the opportunity to expand their product offerings. For start-ups, M&A can provide access to capital, resources, and expertise that may not be available otherwise. M&A can provide a platform for start-ups to quickly scale their business and expand their customer base.

M&A can also help businesses develop and grow in other ways. For example, M&A can help businesses reduce costs by eliminating redundant operations and personnel, and it can help businesses increase efficiency by combining operations and streamlining processes. M&A can help businesses gain access to new markets, technologies, and resources, as well as the opportunity to expand their product offerings.

M&A is a powerful tool for both established companies and start-ups. It can provide access to new markets, technologies, and resources, as well as the opportunity to expand its product offerings. M&A can help businesses reduce costs, increase efficiency, and gain access to new markets.

Small Business Administration Loans

The Small Business Administration (SBA) is a federal agency that provides assistance to small businesses in the United States. The SBA offers a variety of loan programs to help small businesses start, grow, and succeed. These loans can be used for a variety of purposes, including business expansion, equipment purchases, working capital, and debt refinancing.

The SBA loan programs are designed to help small businesses access capital that may not be available through traditional financing sources. The SBA does not directly lend money to businesses but instead guarantees loans made by participating lenders. This helps to reduce the risk for lenders and makes it easier for small businesses to qualify for financing.

The SBA offers several loan programs, including the 7(a) Loan Program, the 504 Loan Program, and the Microloan Program. The 7(a) Loan Program is the most popular SBA loan program and is used for a variety of purposes, including business expansion, equipment purchases, working capital, and debt refinancing. The 504 Loan Program is designed to help small businesses purchase fixed assets, such as real estate and equipment. The Microloan Program provides small loans of up to $50,000 to help small businesses start up and expand.

The SBA loan programs provide a number of benefits to small businesses. The loans are typically easier to qualify for than traditional bank loans, and they often have lower interest rates and longer repayment terms. The SBA also offers free counseling and training to help small business owners understand the loan process and manage their businesses.

Convertible Debt

Convertible debt is a type of loan that can be converted into equity at a later date. It is a popular form of financing for start-ups and other businesses that need capital but don't have the assets or credit history to qualify for traditional bank loans. Convertible debt is attractive to investors because it offers them the potential for a higher return on their investment.

Convertible debt is a great way for businesses to get the capital they need to grow and develop. It can provide the funds needed to develop new products, hire new employees, and expand operations. It also allows businesses to avoid the high-interest rates associated with traditional loans.

Convertible debt can also be beneficial for start-ups because it allows them to raise capital without giving up any equity in their company. This is especially attractive to entrepreneurs who want to retain control of their businesses.

Convertible debt can also be used to bridge the gap between seed funding and a Series A round of financing. This is especially helpful for start-ups that need additional capital to reach the next level of growth.

Convertible debt can be a sure way for businesses to get the capital they need to grow and develop. It is used to bridge the gap between seed funding and a Series A round of financing.

Revenue-Based Financing

- Revenue-based financing (RBF) is a type of financing that allows businesses to borrow money based on their current and future revenue. RBF is an alternative to traditional debt financing and equity financing, and it is often used by businesses that are unable to access traditional financing. RBF can be a great option for businesses that need capital quickly and don't want to take on the risk of equity financing.

- RBF is a form of debt financing that is based on a company's current and future revenue. Unlike traditional debt financing, RBF does not require collateral or a credit score. Instead, the lender looks at the company's revenue and cash flow to determine the amount of money they are willing to lend. The lender will also look at the company's growth potential and financial history to determine the repayment terms.

- RBF is a great option for businesses that need capital quickly and don't want to take on the risk of equity financing. RBF can provide businesses with the capital they need to grow and expand without having to give up any ownership or control of the company. RBF is used to finance short-term projects or investments, such as marketing campaigns or new product launches.

- RBF is a great option for businesses that are just starting out. It can provide businesses with the capital they need to get off the ground without having to give up any ownership or control of the company. RBF can be used to finance short-term projects or investments, such as marketing campaigns or new product launches.

Private Placement

Private placements are a form of financing that involves the sale of securities to a limited number of investors, usually without the need for registration with the Securities and Exchange Commission (SEC). Private placements are often used by companies to raise capital for business development and expansion.

Private placements can be good for start-ups and small businesses to raise capital quickly and efficiently. They can be used to finance new projects, expand existing operations, or acquire other businesses. Private placements are also attractive to investors because they typically offer higher returns than other forms of financing.

Private placements are typically offered to accredited investors, which are individuals or entities that meet certain financial thresholds. These investors must be able to demonstrate that they have the financial resources and knowledge to understand the risks associated with the investment.

Private placements are structured in a variety of ways, including debt, equity, or a combination of both. Companies can also offer different types of securities, such as common stock, preferred stock, or convertible debt.

Private placements can provide start-ups and small businesses with access to capital that may not be available through traditional financing sources. They also provide investors with the opportunity to invest in a company at an early stage and potentially realize higher returns than they would with other investments.

Private placements can also be used to raise capital for specific projects or initiatives, such as research and development, marketing, or acquisitions. Companies can also use private placements to restructure their debt or equity capital structure.

Private placements are supported for start-ups and small businesses to raise capital quickly and efficiently. They can also provide investors with the opportunity to invest in a company

Asset-Based Lending

- Asset-based lending (ABL) is a type of financing that uses a company's assets as collateral for a loan. It is a popular form of financing for businesses that need quick access to capital and don't have access to traditional sources of financing.

ABL is used to finance a wide range of business activities, including working capital, expansion, acquisitions, and more.

- ABL can be used to finance a wide range of business activities, including working capital, expansion, acquisitions, and more. ABL is an attractive option for businesses that have difficulty obtaining traditional financing. It is a flexible form of financing that can be tailored to meet the needs of the business. ABL can provide businesses with the funds they need to grow.

- ABL is a great option for start-ups and small businesses that need capital to get off the ground. ABL can provide the funds needed to purchase equipment, hire staff, and purchase inventory. It is used to finance expansion and acquisitions.

- ABL is also used to finance mergers and acquisitions and to provide the capital needed to finance the purchase of another company or to finance the merger of two companies. it is used to finance restructuring and turnarounds to provide the capital needed to restructure a business and make it more profitable. Asset-based lending is a great option for businesses that need quick access to capital.

Leasing

Leasing is a form of financing that allows businesses to acquire assets without having to pay the full purchase price upfront. It is a popular option for businesses of all sizes, from start-ups to large corporations, as it provides them with access to the equipment, they need to operate without having to spend a large amount of capital.

Leasing can have a significant impact on business growth and start-up success. By allowing businesses to acquire assets without having to pay the full purchase price upfront, leasing provides them with the capital they need to invest in other areas of their business, such as marketing, research and development, and hiring additional employees. This can help businesses grow and expand, as well as increase their chances of success.

Leasing also provides businesses with more flexibility than traditional financing options. For example, businesses can choose the length of the lease, the payment terms, and the type of asset they are leasing. This allows businesses to tailor their leasing agreement to their specific needs and budget.

Leasing can help businesses manage their cash flow. By spreading out the cost of the asset over the term of the lease, businesses can avoid having to pay a large sum of money upfront. This can help businesses manage their cash flow and ensure that they have enough money to cover their other expenses.

Leasing is a great option for businesses of all sizes, from start-ups to large corporations. It can provide businesses with the capital they need to invest in other areas of their business, as well as more flexibility and better cash flow management. By taking advantage of leasing, businesses can increase their chances of success and help ensure their long-term growth and success.

Trade Credit

Trade credit is a form of financing that allows businesses to purchase goods or services without having to pay for them immediately. It is a type of short-term financing that is extended to a business by its suppliers or vendors. The supplier or vendor agrees to provide goods or services to the business and allows the business to pay for them at a later date. This type of financing is often used by businesses to purchase inventory, cover operational costs, or fund growth   initiatives.

Trade credit is an important source of financing for businesses, particularly for start-ups and small businesses. It can provide access to capital that may not be available from traditional sources, such as banks or investors. Trade credit can also help businesses manage their cash flow by allowing them to purchase goods and services without having to pay for them immediately. This is especially beneficial for businesses that are experiencing seasonal fluctuations in sales or have limited access to other forms of financing.

Trade credit can also help businesses grow and expand. By allowing businesses to purchase goods and services without having to pay for them immediately, trade credit can help businesses purchase inventory or invest in new equipment that can help them increase production and sales. This can help businesses increase their revenues and profits, which can lead to further growth and expansion.

Trade credit can also be beneficial for start-ups. Start-ups often have limited access to capital and may not be able to secure financing from traditional sources. Trade credit can provide a source of financing that can help start-ups purchase inventory and invest in new equipment, which can help them get their business off the ground.

Trade credit is an important source of financing for businesses, particularly for start-ups and small businesses.

Supplier Financing

Supplier financing is a type of financing where is the supplier finance the business to purchase goods or services from the supplier. This type of financing is beneficial for businesses that need to purchase goods or services but do not have the necessary funds to do so. It can also be beneficial for start-ups, as it can help them to acquire the necessary goods or services to get their business off the ground.

Supplier financing can have a positive impact on business growth and start-up success. By providing access to goods and services that may otherwise be out of reach, supplier financing can help businesses to expand their operations and increase their revenue. This is especially beneficial for start-ups, as it can help them to acquire the necessary resources to get their business off the ground. Supplier financing can help businesses to manage their cash flow more effectively, as they can purchase goods and services on credit and then pay for them over time. This can help businesses to better manage their finances and ensure that they have the necessary funds to cover their expenses.

In addition to helping businesses to acquire the necessary resources to grow, supplier financing can also help to reduce the risk associated with purchasing goods or services. By allowing businesses to purchase goods and services on credit, supplier financing can help to reduce the risk of not being able to pay for goods or services that have already been purchased. This can help businesses to avoid financial losses due to non-payment and can help them to better manage their finances.

Supplier financing is a beneficial tool for businesses and start-ups. It can help businesses to acquire the necessary resources to grow and can help start-ups to get their business off the ground. It can help businesses to better manage their cash flow and reduce the risk associated

Note:

Trade credit is a short-term loan extended to a customer by a supplier, allowing the customer to purchase goods or services and pay for them at a later date.

Supplier financing is a type of financing arrangement where a supplier provides a loan to a customer to help finance the purchase of goods or services. The supplier may require the customer to make regular payments or may require the customer to pay the entire loan amount at the end of the agreement. The supplier may also require collateral or a personal guarantee from the customer.

Export Financing

Export financing is a type of financing that helps businesses and start-ups to finance their export activities. It is a form of credit that helps businesses to cover the costs associated with exporting goods and services, such as transportation, insurance, and customs duties. Export financing is used to cover the costs of production, marketing, and other activities related to exporting.

Export financing can have a significant impact on business growth and start-ups. One of the main benefits of export financing is that it provides businesses with access to capital that they may not be able to access through traditional financing methods. This is especially beneficial for start-ups, as they often lack the collateral or credit history to qualify for traditional financing. Export financing can also help businesses to expand their operations and reach new markets, which can lead to increased sales and profits.

Export financing can also help businesses to manage their cash flow more effectively. By providing businesses with access to capital, export financing can help businesses to cover their expenses and pay for goods and services in a timely manner. This can help businesses to avoid costly delays in production or delivery, which can have a negative impact on their bottom line.

By providing businesses with access to capital, export financing can help businesses to build relationships with foreign buyers, which can lead to increased sales and profits.

Joint Ventures

A joint venture (JV) is a business arrangement in which two or more parties agree to combine their resources in order to achieve a specific goal. Joint ventures are often used by companies to expand their operations, enter new markets, and gain access to new technologies. They can also be used by start-ups to access capital, resources, and expertise that would otherwise be unavailable.

Joint ventures offer a number of advantages for businesses and start-ups. By combining resources, companies can reduce costs and risks associated with entering new markets or launching new products.

They can also gain access to new technologies and expertise that would otherwise be unavailable.

Joint ventures can provide start-ups with a platform to test and validate their products and services in the market.

Furthermore, joint ventures can provide a platform for companies to collaborate and innovate, which can lead to increased efficiency and productivity.

Strategic Partnerships

Strategic partnerships are an important tool for businesses of all sizes to grow and succeed. Strategic partnerships allow businesses to leverage the resources, expertise, and networks of other organizations to create new opportunities and increase their competitive advantage. Strategic partnerships can be formed between two or more companies, between a company and a government agency, or between a company and an educational institution. Strategic partnerships can help businesses expand their customer base, increase their market share, and develop new products and services. They can also help start-ups gain access to capital, resources, and expertise to launch their business.

A strategic partnership is a formal agreement between two or more organizations to work together to achieve a common goal. Strategic partnerships are formed when two or more organizations have complementary strengths and resources that can be leveraged to create a competitive advantage.

Strategic partnerships can help businesses expand their customer base and increase their market share. By leveraging the resources and networks of other organizations, businesses can reach new customers and markets that they may not have been able to reach on their own.

Strategic partnerships can provide businesses with access to resources, such as capital, technology, and expertise, that they may not have had access to on their own. This is especially beneficial for start-ups, which often lack the resources to launch their business.

Strategic partnerships can provide a number of benefits to businesses of all sizes. These benefits include:

- **Access to New Resources**: Strategic partnerships provide access to new resources such as technology, capital, and expertise that can help a business grow.

- **Increased Market Reach**: Strategic partnerships can help a business expand its reach into new markets and customer segments.

- **Cost Savings**: Strategic partnerships can help a business reduce costs by sharing resources and leveraging economies of scale.

- **Risk Mitigation**: Strategic partnerships can help a business reduce risk by sharing the burden of risk and spreading it across multiple partners.

- **Increased Efficiency**: Strategic partnerships can help a business become more efficient by sharing resources and leveraging each other's strengths.

- **Increased Innovation**: Strategic partnerships can help a business become more innovative by combining ideas and resources from different partners.

- **Improved Brand Recognition**: Strategic partnerships can help a business increase its brand recognition by leveraging the partner's brand.

- **Access to Talent**: Strategic partnerships can help a business access new talent and skillsets that can help it grow.

- **Increased Customer Loyalty**: Strategic partnerships can help a business increase customer loyalty by providing customers with better service and more value.

- **Improved Competitiveness**: Strategic partnerships can help a business become more competitive by leveraging the partner's strengths and resources.

Investment Banks

An investment bank is a financial institution that provides a range of services to businesses, governments, and individuals. Investment banks specialize in underwriting and issuing securities, providing advice on mergers and acquisitions, and providing other financial services. Investment banks play a critical role in the economy by providing capital to businesses and helping them to grow. They also provide advice and guidance to start-ups and other businesses looking to expand.

Investment banks play a key role in the growth of businesses. They provide capital to businesses in the form of debt and equity financing. This capital is used to fund expansion, research and development, and acquisitions. Investment banks also provide advice and guidance to businesses on how to best use their capital and how to structure their finances. This advice is invaluable in helping businesses to grow and succeed.

Investment banks also provide advice on mergers and acquisitions. They can help businesses to identify potential acquisition targets and provide advice on how to structure the deal. This is beneficial for businesses looking to expand their operations or enter new markets.

Investment banks can also play a key role in helping start-ups to grow and succeed. They can provide capital to start-ups in the form of venture capital or debt financing. This capital is used to fund research and development, marketing, and other activities. Investment banks can also provide advice and guidance on how to structure the business and how to best use the capital. This advice is invaluable for start-ups as they look to grow and succeed.

Investment banks play a critical role in the economy by providing capital to businesses and helping them grow.

Credit Unions

Credit unions are a type of financial institution that provides banking services to members who share a common bond, such as a place of employment, or a community. Credit unions are not-for-profit organizations that are owned and operated by their members. They offer a variety of services, including savings accounts, checking accounts, loans, and other financial services.

Credit unions have a long history of providing financial services to their members, and they have become increasingly popular in recent years as an alternative to traditional banks. Credit unions offer many advantages to their members, including lower fees, lower interest rates, and more personalized service.

Credit unions have a positive impact on business growth and start-ups. Credit unions provide access to capital for businesses, which is used to fund new projects, hire new employees, and purchase equipment. Credit unions also offer lower interest rates on loans than traditional banks, making it easier for businesses to access the capital they need to grow.

Credit unions also provide access to financial education and advice to their members, which is beneficial to businesses. Credit unions often offer seminars and workshops on topics such as budgeting, credit management, and business planning. This can help businesses make more informed decisions about their finances and can help them make better use of their   resources.

Credit unions also provide a sense of community and support to their members. Credit unions often host events and activities that bring members together and provide a sense of camaraderie. This is beneficial for businesses, as it can help foster relationships between members and create a network of potential customers   and   partners.

Credit unions have a positive impact on business growth and start-ups. They provide access to capital.

Community Development Financial Institutions

Community Development Financial Institutions (CDFIs) are specialized financial institutions that provide access to capital and financial services to underserved populations and communities. CDFIs are typically non-profit organizations that are certified by the U.S. Department of the Treasury. They provide capital to small businesses, entrepreneurs, and low-income communities that may not have access to traditional banking services. CDFIs have become increasingly important in providing access to capital and financial services to underserved populations and communities.

CDFIs provide access to capital and financial services to entrepreneurs, small businesses, and low-income communities that may not have access to traditional banking services. This access to capital and financial services can help businesses grow and expand. CDFIs also provide technical assistance and business training to help entrepreneurs and small businesses succeed. This assistance can help businesses develop and implement effective business plans, access capital, and manage their finances.

Start-ups and small businesses often lack access to traditional banking services and capital. CDFIs can provide access to capital to help start-ups and small businesses get off the ground and grow. This access to capital can help businesses expand, hire more employees, and increase their revenues.

Mezzanine Financing

Mezzanine financing is a form of capital that is used to finance business growth and start-ups. It is a hybrid of debt and equity financing and is typically used when traditional debt financing is not available or not sufficient. Mezzanine financing is a popular form of financing for start-ups and small businesses because it is relatively easy to obtain and provides flexible terms.

Mezzanine financing is typically structured as a loan with a higher interest rate than a traditional loan. The loan is secured by the company's assets, but the lender also receives an equity stake in the company. This equity stake gives the lender a greater level of control over the company's operations. The equity stake also provides the lender with the potential for a greater return on their investment if the company is successful.

Mezzanine financing is an opportunity to finance business growth and start-ups. It provides the company with the capital it needs to expand and grow, while also providing the lender with the potential for a greater return on their investment. The flexibility of the terms and the ability to obtain financing quickly make it an attractive option for many   businesses.

Mezzanine financing can also be beneficial to start-ups. It can provide the capital needed to launch a business, and the equity stake gives the lender a greater level of control over the company's operations. This is beneficial to start-ups because it can provide the lender with the assurance that the company   is   being   managed   properly.

Mezzanine financing is a wonderful process to finance business growth and start-ups. It provides the company with the capital it needs to expand and grow.

Royalty Financing

Royalty financing is a form of capital investment that allows a company to receive upfront capital from investors in exchange for a percentage of future sales. This type of financing is beneficial for both the company and the investor, as it provides the company with the capital it needs to grow and the investor with a return on their investment.

Royalty financing is a great option for start-ups and small businesses that need capital but don't have the financial resources to secure traditional financing. It allows them to receive upfront capital without having to give up equity or take on additional debt. This type of financing also allows the company to maintain control over its business, as they are not required to give up any ownership or control to the investor.

Royalty financing can also be beneficial for investors, as it provides them with a steady stream of income. The investor receives a percentage of the company's sales, which is a great source of passive income. This type of financing also allows investors to diversify their portfolio, as they can invest in multiple companies and receive a return on their investment without having to take on additional risk.

The impact of royalty financing on business growth and start-ups is significant. By providing companies with the capital, they need to grow. Royalty financing can help them expand their operations and increase their revenue. This can lead to increased profits and a larger market share, which can help the company become more competitive in its industry.

For start-ups, royalty financing can provide the capital they need to get their business off the ground. It can help them launch their product or service and get it to market faster, allowing them to start generating revenue sooner. This can give them a competitive edge

Social Impact Bonds

Social Impact Bonds (SIBs) are a new form of financing that has emerged in recent years as a way to fund social programs. They are a type of public-private partnership that allows private investors to fund social programs in exchange for a return on their investment if the program is successful. SIBs are designed to help governments and non-profits finance innovative social programs that have the potential to improve the lives of citizens and communities.

The idea behind SIBs is that private investors provide the upfront capital to fund a social program, and then receive a return on their investment if the program is successful. This return is based on the outcomes of the program, such as reduced crime rates or improved educational outcomes. If the program is successful, the government or non-profit organization pays back the investors with a return on their investment.

SIBs have the potential to be a powerful tool for

governments and non-profits to fund innovative social programs. They can be used to fund programs that may not be eligible for traditional government funding, such as programs that focus on improving educational outcomes. They also provide an incentive for private investors to fund programs that may not be attractive to traditional investors.

SIBs have the potential to be a powerful tool for business growth and start-ups. By providing a source of capital for innovative social programs, SIBs can help start-ups and small businesses access the capital they need to grow and succeed. SIBs can also provide an incentive for investors to invest in start-ups and small businesses, as they can receive a return on their investment if the program is successful.

Corporate Sponsorships

Corporate sponsorships are an increasingly popular way for businesses to gain visibility and recognition in the marketplace. A corporate sponsorship is an agreement between a company and an organization or individual, in which the company provides financial or other support in exchange for the organization or individual's endorsement of the company's products or services. Corporate sponsorships can range from small local events to large national campaigns.

The primary benefit of corporate sponsorships is increased visibility and brand recognition. By sponsoring an event or organization, companies can reach a wide audience and create a positive image for their brand. This can lead to increased sales and customer loyalty. In addition, corporate sponsorships can help to build relationships with customers, partners, and other stakeholders.

Corporate sponsorships can also have a positive impact on business growth and start-ups. By sponsoring an event or organization, businesses can gain access to new customers and potential partners. This can lead to increased sales and revenue, as well as increased market share. Corporate sponsorships can help to build relationships with potential investors and partners, which can lead to increased funding and resources.

Corporate sponsorships can help to create a positive public image for businesses. By sponsoring an event or organization, businesses can demonstrate their commitment to the community and their willingness to support causes that are important to their customers. This can help to build trust and loyalty among customers, which can lead to increased sales and customer loyalty.

In conclusion, corporate sponsorships can have a positive impact on business growth and start-ups. By providing financial or other support in exchange for the organization or individual's endorsement of the company's products or services, businesses can gain increased visibility, brand recognition, and access to new customers.

Online Fundraising Platforms

Online fundraising platforms have become increasingly popular in recent years, as they provide an easy and efficient way for entrepreneurs and businesses to raise money for their projects. Online fundraising platforms allow entrepreneurs and businesses to reach a larger audience, and to raise more money than traditional fundraising methods.

Online fundraising platforms have had a significant impact on business growth. These platforms allow businesses to reach a larger audience than traditional fundraising methods, which can result in more money being raised. Online fundraising platforms are often more cost-effective than traditional methods, as they require less time and effort to set up and manage. This can result in businesses being able to save money and invest it in other areas of their business.

Furthermore, online fundraising platforms can help businesses to build relationships with their donors. These platforms allow businesses to communicate with their donors and provide them with updates on their progress. This can help to build trust between the business and its donors, which can result in more donations in the future.

Online fundraising platforms are often more cost-effective than traditional methods, as they require less time and effort to set up and manage. This can help start-ups to save money and invest it in other areas of their business.

Local Business Organizations

Local business organizations are organizations that are formed by local businesses and entrepreneurs to promote the growth of businesses in their local area. These organizations can provide a variety of services and resources to help businesses grow and succeed. They can provide access to funding, mentorship, networking opportunities, business advice, resources, and more.

The impact of local business organizations on business growth and start-ups is significant. These organizations provide a platform for businesses to connect and collaborate with each other, which can lead to increased innovation and growth. They can also provide access to resources and advice that can help businesses to succeed.

Local business organizations can also help to create a sense of community among businesses in the local area. This can lead to increased collaboration and networking opportunities, which can help to drive business growth. They can also provide access to funding, which is invaluable for start-ups and small businesses.

Local business organizations can also help to promote the local economy. By providing resources and advice to businesses, they can help to create jobs and stimulate economic growth. This can have a positive impact on the local area, as businesses are able to grow and contribute to the local economy.

In conclusion, local business organizations can have a

significant impact on business growth and start-ups. They can provide access to resources, advice, and funding, as well as create a sense of community among businesses in the local area. This can help to drive business growth and stimulate economic growth in the local area.

Local Banks

Local banks play a vital role in the economic growth of a region. They provide financial services to individuals, businesses, and organizations, and help to stimulate economic growth by providing access to capital. Local banks also provide a variety of services to businesses, such as business loans, lines of credit, and merchant services. These services can be invaluable for businesses, particularly start-ups, as they provide access to capital and the ability to manage cash flow.

Local banks have a significant impact on business growth. They provide access to capital, which is essential for businesses to grow and expand. Businesses can use the capital provided by local banks to purchase equipment, hire new employees, and open new locations. Local banks provide a variety of services to businesses, such as business loans, lines of credit, and merchant services. These services can help businesses manage their cash flow, and can be invaluable for start-ups, as they provide access to capital and the ability to manage cash flow.

Local banks can be particularly beneficial for start-ups. Start-ups often have limited access to capital, and local banks can provide the necessary capital to help them get off the ground.

Local Investors

Local investors can have a significant impact on the growth of businesses and start-ups. Local investors are individuals or organizations that invest in businesses or start-ups within their local area. They can provide capital, resources, and expertise to help businesses and start-ups grow and succeed.

The benefits of local investors are numerous. Local investors can provide capital to businesses and start-ups that may not be able to access traditional sources of funding. They can also provide advice and guidance to help businesses and start-ups make better decisions. Local investors can provide access to networks and resources that can help businesses and start-ups grow.

Local investors can also have a positive impact on the local economy. By investing in local businesses and start-ups, local investors can help create jobs, spur economic growth, and generate tax revenue. This can help create a more vibrant and prosperous local economy.

Local investors can also help foster innovation and entrepreneurship. By investing in local businesses and start-ups, local investors can help create an environment that encourages innovation and entrepreneurship. This can lead to the development of new products and services, which can create new jobs and economic opportunities.

Local investors can help create a sense of community. By investing in local businesses and start-ups, local investors can help create a sense of pride and ownership in the local community. This can help create a stronger sense of community and can help foster a more vibrant local economy.

Regional Investment Funds

Regional Investment Funds (RIFs) are a type of venture capital fund that invests in businesses located in a specific region. RIFs are typically managed by a professional investment firm and are designed to provide capital to businesses in the region in order to stimulate economic growth and job creation. RIFs are often used to finance start-ups and small businesses that may not be able to access traditional sources of capital.

The impact of RIFs on business growth and start-ups can be significant. RIFs provide access to capital that may not be available from traditional sources, such as banks or venture capital firms. This is especially beneficial for start-ups and small businesses that may not have the resources to access capital from other sources. RIFs can provide a source of capital for businesses that may not have the collateral or credit history to secure a loan from a bank.

RIFs can also provide businesses with access to experienced investors and advisors who can provide guidance and advice on how to best use the capital to grow the business. This is especially beneficial for start-ups and small businesses that may not have access to experienced advisors.

RIFs can also help to create jobs in the region. By investing in businesses in the region, RIFs can help to create new jobs and stimulate economic growth. This is especially beneficial for regions that may be struggling economically.

RIFs can have a significant impact on business growth and start-ups. By providing access to capital and experienced advisors, RIFs can help businesses to grow and create jobs in the region.

Regional Development Banks

Regional Development Banks (RDBs) are specialized financial institutions that provide loans, grants, and other financial assistance to businesses and individuals in a particular region. RDBs are typically established by governments to promote economic development in a specific region, and to provide access to capital for businesses and individuals who may not otherwise have access to traditional sources of financing.

RDBs have a significant impact on business growth and start-ups. By providing access to capital, RDBs enable businesses to expand their operations and hire additional employees. This increased economic activity can lead to job creation, increased wages, and increased economic growth in the region. RDBs can provide technical assistance and advice to businesses, which can help them become more competitive and successful.

RDBs also provide financing to start-ups, which is critical to the success of a new business. Start-ups often lack the capital needed to launch their business, and RDBs can provide the necessary funds to get the business off the ground. RDBs can provide advice and guidance to start-ups, which can help them navigate the complexities of starting a business.

RDBs can provide access to capital to individuals who may not otherwise have access to traditional sources of financing. This is especially beneficial for individuals who are in lower-income brackets or who have poor credit histories. By providing access to capital, RDBs can help individuals start businesses, purchase homes, and finance other important investments.

Community Investment Funds

Community Investment Funds (CIFs) are a type of financial instrument that provides capital to businesses and start-ups in underserved communities. These funds are designed to help spur economic development and job creation in areas that are often overlooked by traditional lenders. CIFs are typically funded by public and private sources, including government grants, foundations, and corporate investments.

The primary goal of CIFs is to provide capital to

businesses and start-ups in underserved communities, allowing them to grow and create jobs. This type of investment can have a positive impact on the local economy, as businesses are able to expand and hire more employees. CIFs can help to reduce poverty and inequality in the community by providing access to capital for those who may not otherwise have access to traditional financing.

CIFs can also provide a boost to start-ups and small businesses. By providing capital to these businesses, CIFs can help them to grow and become more competitive in their respective markets. This can lead to increased sales and profits, which can in turn lead to more jobs and economic growth in the community.

CIFs can also help to attract new businesses to the area. By providing capital to start-ups and small businesses, CIFs can help to create a more attractive business environment in the community. This can attract new businesses and entrepreneurs, which can lead to increased economic activity and job creation.

Public Investment Funds

Public Investment Funds (PIFs) are government-sponsored investment vehicles that are used to finance public projects and stimulate economic growth. PIFs are typically managed by a government agency or a private entity, and they can be used to finance a variety of projects, including infrastructure, housing, education, health care, and technology.

The primary purpose of PIFs is to stimulate economic

growth and development in a region or country. By investing in public projects, PIFs can help create jobs, attract new businesses, and generate revenue for the government. PIFs can help to reduce poverty and inequality by providing access to capital for those who are unable to access traditional financing.

PIFs can have a significant impact on business growth and start-ups. By providing access to capital, PIFs can help entrepreneurs and small businesses get off the ground and expand. PIFs can also provide access to new markets and technologies, which can help businesses grow and become more competitive. PIFs can provide access to technical assistance and mentorship, which can help businesses develop and succeed.

PIFs can also have an impact on the local economy. By investing in local projects, PIFs can help to create jobs and stimulate economic activity. PIFs can help to attract new businesses and investments to the area, which can lead to increased economic growth.

Government-Backed Loans

Government-backed loans are loans that are issued by banks or other financial institutions and are backed by a government guarantee. These loans are designed to help businesses grow and start-ups get off the ground. The government provides a guarantee to the lender that the loan will be repaid, even if the business fails. This reduces the risk for the lender, making them more likely to approve the loan.

Government-backed loans are beneficial for businesses because they typically have lower interest rates than traditional loans. This makes them more affordable for businesses, allowing them to access the capital they need to grow and expand. These loans often have more flexible repayment terms, making them easier to manage.

Government-backed loans can also help businesses access capital that they may not be able to get from traditional lenders. This is especially true for start-ups, which often lack the necessary credit history or collateral to secure a loan from a bank. Government-backed loans can provide the necessary capital to get a business off the ground.

The availability of government-backed loans can also have a positive impact on the economy. By providing businesses with access to capital, these loans can help create jobs and spur economic growth. The lower interest rates associated with these loans can help businesses save money, which can be reinvested in the business or used to hire more employees.

Small Business Investment Companies

Small Business Investment Companies (SBICs) are private venture capital firms that provide capital and assistance to small businesses. These companies are licensed and regulated by the Small Business Administration (SBA) and are designed to help small businesses grow and expand. SBICs provide a variety of services, including venture capital, debt financing, and management assistance.

SBICs provide a valuable source of capital for small businesses, especially those that are unable to obtain financing from traditional sources. SBICs can provide a variety of financing options, including equity investments, debt financing, and venture capital. SBICs also provide management assistance, such as strategic planning, market research, and business development services.

The impact of SBICs on business growth and start-ups is significant. SBICs provide a source of capital that is often not available to small businesses from traditional sources. This capital allows small businesses to expand their operations, hire additional employees, and purchase new equipment. In addition, the management assistance provided by SBICs can help small businesses develop effective strategies for growth and success.

SBICs also provide a valuable source of capital for start-ups. Start-ups often lack the capital needed to launch their business and grow. SBICs can provide the necessary capital to help start-ups get off the ground and grow. In addition, the management assistance provided by SBICs can help start-ups develop effective strategies for growth and success.

Subordinated Debt

Subordinated debt is a type of debt that ranks lower in priority than other debt obligations in the event of a company's liquidation. It is also known as junior debt or subordinated loan. Subordinated debt is typically unsecured and carries higher interest rates than other forms of debt.

Subordinated debt is a useful tool for businesses to raise capital. It provides a source of financing that is not as expensive as equity and is used to finance a variety of activities, such as expansion, acquisitions, and refinancing. Subordinated debt can also be used to increase the leverage of a company, which can help to increase returns to shareholders.

Subordinated debt is beneficial for start-ups as it can help them to secure financing without having to give up equity in the company. It can also be used to finance activities that would otherwise be too costly for the company to finance with equity.

Subordinated debt can also be beneficial for businesses looking to grow. It can provide a source of financing that is not as expensive as equity and is used to finance activities such as expansion, acquisitions, and refinancing. The use of subordinated debt can also help to increase the leverage of a company, which can help to increase returns to shareholders.

Subordinated debt can also help to reduce the risk of a company's failure. In the event of a company's liquidation, subordinated debt holders are paid after other creditors, which can help to reduce the risk of losses for the company.

Tax Increment Financing

Tax Increment Financing (TIF) is a public financing tool used to fund public infrastructure and development projects. It is a way for local governments to finance projects that would otherwise be too expensive to fund through traditional means. TIF is used to attract private investment and stimulate economic growth in a specific area.

TIF works by allowing a local government to capture the increased property tax revenue generated by a development project and use it to finance the project. The increased property tax revenue is known as the "tax increment" and is the difference between the amount of property tax revenue generated before the project and the amount generated after the project is completed.

TIF is an attractive financing option for businesses because it allows them to access funds for projects without having to take on additional debt. This is especially beneficial for start-ups and small businesses that may not have access to traditional financing options.

TIF can also be used to fund public infrastructure projects such as roads, bridges, and public transportation. These projects can help create a more attractive environment for businesses, which can lead to increased economic growth and job creation.

TIF can also be used to fund public services such as schools, libraries, and parks. These services can help create a more attractive environment for businesses, which can lead to increased economic growth and job creation.

Unsecured Business Loans

Unsecured business loans are a type of financing that does not require collateral to be used as security. They are often used by small businesses and start-ups to finance their operations and growth.

The main advantage of unsecured business loans is that they are easier to obtain than secured loans. This is because the lender does not have to worry about the borrower defaulting on the loan, as there is no collateral to repossess in the event of a default. This makes them attractive to businesses that may not have the assets to secure a loan.

Another advantage of unsecured business loans is that they can provide businesses with access to capital quickly. This is especially beneficial for start-ups, as they often need access to funds quickly to get their business off the ground.

The downside of unsecured business loans is that they tend to have higher interest rates than secured loans. This is because the lender is taking on more risk by not having any collateral to repossess in the event of a default.

In addition, unsecured business loans are difficult to obtain. This is because lenders are often hesitant to lend money to businesses that don't have any assets to   secure   the   loan.

Despite the higher interest rates and difficulty in obtaining them, unsecured business loans are good for businesses to access capital quickly. This is especially beneficial for start-ups, as they often need access to funds quickly to get their business off the ground.

USDA Business Loans

The United States Department of Agriculture (USDA) provides business loans to small businesses and start-ups in rural areas. These loans are designed to help businesses grow and expand, create jobs, and improve the local economy. The USDA provides both direct and guaranteed loans to businesses, and the terms and conditions vary depending on the type of loan.

Direct loans are provided directly from the USDA to the business. These loans are typically used for business expansion, equipment purchases, and working capital. The terms of the loan can vary, but typically include a fixed interest rate and repayment terms of up to 30 years. The amount of the loan is based on the borrower's creditworthiness and the purpose   of   the   loan.

Guaranteed loans are provided by private lenders, but are backed by the USDA. These loans are typically used for business start-ups and expansions, and the terms and conditions of the loan are determined by the lender. The amount of the loan is based on the borrower's creditworthiness and the purpose of the loan.

The USDA business loan program has had a positive impact on businesses and start-ups in rural areas. These loans have allowed businesses to expand and create jobs, which has helped to improve the local economy. The loans have also allowed businesses to purchase equipment and working capital, which has helped them to become more competitive and profitable.

Vendor Financing

Vendor financing is a type of financing that is provided by a vendor or supplier to a customer. It is a form of short-term financing that is used to purchase goods or services from a vendor or supplier. Vendor financing is often used by businesses to purchase inventory, equipment, or other goods and services from a vendor or supplier.

Vendor financing is beneficial to both the vendor and the customer. For the vendor, it can provide a steady stream of income and help to build customer loyalty. For the customer, it can provide access to needed goods and services without having to pay upfront. This is especially beneficial for small businesses and start-ups, who may not have the resources to pay for large purchases upfront.

Vendor financing can have a positive impact on

business growth and start-ups. Providing access to needed goods and services without having to pay upfront, can help to reduce costs and increase cash flow. This can help businesses to grow and expand, as well as allow them to take advantage of opportunities that may not have been available without the financing.

Vendor financing can also be beneficial for start-ups. Providing access to needed goods and services without having to pay upfront, can help to reduce costs and increase cash flow. This can help start-ups to get off the ground and start generating revenue. It can also help to build customer loyalty, as customers may be more likely to purchase from a vendor that provides financing.

Women's Business Centres

Women's Business Centres (WBCs) are a type of business incubator that provides resources and support to female entrepreneurs. WBCs are designed to help women start, grow, and sustain their businesses. They provide a range of services, including business plan development, financial literacy, access to capital, mentorship, and networking opportunities. WBCs also provide access to resources such as market research, business coaching, and legal advice.

The impact of WBCs on business growth and start-ups is significant. WBCs provide the resources and support needed for women to start and grow their businesses. They provide access to capital, mentorship, and networking opportunities, which is invaluable for entrepreneurs. WBCs also provide access to resources such as market research, business coaching, and legal advice, which can help entrepreneurs make informed decisions and increase their chances of success.

WBCs have also been shown to have a positive impact on the economic growth of communities. Studies have found that WBCs have a positive effect on job creation, economic development, and the overall economic health of communities. WBCs have also been found to have a positive effect on the number of women-owned businesses in an area, which can lead to increased economic activity.

Working Capital Loans

Working capital loans are a type of loan that helps businesses cover short-term expenses. These loans are typically used to cover expenses such as payroll, inventory, and other operational costs. Working capital loans are important for businesses as they provide the necessary funds to keep operations running smoothly.

The impact of working capital loans on business growth and start-ups is significant. Working capital loans provide businesses with the funds they need to cover short-term expenses and invest in long-term growth. For start-ups, working capital loans can provide the necessary funds to get the business off the ground. They is used to purchase equipment, hire staff, and cover other start-up costs.

Working capital loans can also help businesses expand and grow. The funds can be used to purchase additional inventory, hire more staff, and invest in marketing and advertising. This can help businesses reach new customers and increase sales. Working capital loans can help businesses manage cash flow and reduce the risk of running out of money.

CHAPTER TWELVE

Utilize Technology to Increase Efficiency

Technology has become an integral part of business operations in the modern world. It has enabled businesses to increase their efficiency and productivity, while also reducing costs. Technology has also enabled businesses to reach new markets and customers, while also providing them with new opportunities to grow and expand.

Technology has had a significant impact on business efficiency. Technology has enabled businesses to automate processes, streamline operations, and reduce costs. Automation has allowed businesses to reduce the time and effort required to complete tasks, while also reducing the need for manual labor. Technology has enabled businesses to access and analyze data more quickly and accurately, allowing them to make better decisions and gain a competitive advantage.

Technology has also enabled businesses to reach new markets and customers. By utilizing digital marketing tools, businesses can reach a wider audience and increase their customer base. Technology has enabled businesses to provide better customer service, which can lead to increased customer loyalty and satisfaction.

Technology has had a significant impact on business growth and start-ups. Technology has enabled businesses to scale quickly and efficiently, while also reducing the cost of doing business. Technology has also enabled businesses to access new markets and customers, while also providing them with new opportunities to grow and expand.

What are the technologies you can use to increase business efficiency?

Automating customer service processes.

- **Automate customer service inquiries:** Use automated chatbots to respond to customer inquiries and provide basic customer service. This can help reduce the number of customer service inquiries and free up time for customer service agents to focus on more complex issues.

- **Automate customer service processes**: Use automation to streamline customer service processes. This can include automating order fulfillment, customer onboarding, and customer feedback. Automating these processes can help reduce manual labor and free up time for customer service agents to focus on more complex issues.

- **Automate customer service analytics:** Use analytics to gain insights into customer service performance. This can help identify areas of improvement and enable customer service agents to better serve customers.

- **Automate customer service feedback:** Use automated feedback systems to collect customer feedback. This can help identify areas of improvement and enable customer service agents to better serve customers.

- **Automate customer service notifications:** Use automated notifications to keep customers informed about their orders, account status, and other important information. This can help reduce customer frustration and improve customer service.

Implementing cloud-based solutions for data storage and sharing.

Cloud-based solutions are becoming increasingly popular for data storage and sharing for business growth and start-ups. Cloud-based solutions offer a number of advantages, including cost savings, scalability, and flexibility. They also provide a secure environment for data storage and sharing.

- **Cost savings:** Cloud-based solutions are often more cost-effective than traditional on-premise solutions. This is because businesses don't need to purchase and maintain expensive hardware or software. Instead, they can pay for the services they need on a pay-as-you-go basis.

- **Scalability:** Cloud-based solutions are highly scalable, meaning businesses can easily increase or decrease their usage depending on their needs. This is particularly useful for start-ups, which may need to quickly scale up their services as their business grows.

- **Flexibility:** Cloud-based solutions are also highly flexible, allowing businesses to access their data from anywhere in the world. This is especially useful for businesses with multiple locations or employees who travel frequently.

- **Security:** Cloud-based solutions are highly secure, as they provide encryption and authentication services to protect data from unauthorized access. This is especially important for businesses that handle sensitive information, such as financial or customer data.

Cloud-based solutions are an ideal choice for businesses looking to store and share data for business growth and start-ups. They offer cost savings, scalability, flexibility, and security, making them a great option for businesses of all sizes.

Using analytics to track customer behavior and preferences.

Analytics is a powerful tool for businesses to track customer behavior and preferences in order to gain insights into customer needs and preferences. This is used to inform decisions about product development, marketing strategies, and customer service.

Businesses can use analytics to track customer behavior and preferences in a number of ways. They can track customer purchase history, website and app usage, and online reviews. This data is used to identify customer needs and preferences, and to develop targeted marketing campaigns and product offerings.

Analytics can also be used to track customer engagement with a company's social media accounts. This can help businesses understand which content resonates with customers and which posts are most likely to generate engagement.

For start-ups, analytics are used to track customer behavior and preferences in order to gain insights into customer needs and preferences. This can help start-ups to identify customer needs and develop products and services that meet those needs. Analytics can also help start-ups to identify potential markets and target them with tailored marketing campaigns.

Online marketing tools to reach new customers.

- **Search Engine Optimization (SEO):** SEO is a powerful tool for getting your business in front of potential customers. It involves optimizing your website and content to rank higher in search engine results, making it easier for customers to find you.

- **Social Media Marketing:** social media is an effective way to reach new customers and build relationships with them. You can use platforms to share content, engage with customers, and promote your business.

- **Content Marketing:** Content marketing is a unique way to attract new customers and build trust with them. You can create blog posts, videos, and other types of content to provide valuable information to your audience and show them why they should choose your business.

- **Email Marketing:** Email marketing is a soft way to stay in touch with existing customers and reach out to new ones. You can use email newsletters to share updates, promotions, and other content to keep customers engaged and interested in your business.

- **Pay-Per-Click Advertising:** Pay-per-click (PPC) advertising is an online way to get your business in front of potential customers quickly. You can use platforms to create ads that target specific keywords and appear when customers search for those terms.

AI-driven chatbots to improve customer service.

AI-driven chatbots can be used to improve customer service for business growth and start-ups in a number of ways. Chatbots are used to automate customer service inquiries, provide personalized customer service, and even provide customer support 24/7.

Chatbots are used to answer customer inquiries quickly and accurately. This can help reduce customer wait times and improve customer satisfaction.

Chatbots can also be used to provide personalized customer service. By using AI-driven natural language processing, chatbots can understand customer inquiries and provide personalized responses.

Chatbots can also be used to provide customer support 24/7. This is especially beneficial for start-ups that may not have the resources to provide customer service around the clock. AI-driven chatbots are used to answer customer inquiries and provide support at any time of the day or night.

AI-driven chatbots are used to collect customer data. This data is used to gain insights into customer behavior and preferences, which can help businesses improve their products and services. By using AI-driven chatbots, businesses can gain valuable insights into their customers and use this data to improve their customer service and grow their business.

Social media platforms to engage with customers.

Social media platforms are a sure way to engage with customers and grow your business. They provide a platform for businesses to interact with their customers, build relationships, and increase brand awareness.

The first step to using social media for business growth is to create a presence on the major social media platforms. This includes setting up accounts on all major social media platforms. Once these accounts are set up, businesses need to start engaging with their customers. This is done through posts, comments, and messages.

Businesses should also use social media to promote their products and services. This is done through posts, ads, and sponsored content. Businesses should use social media to build relationships with their customers. This is done through responding to comments and messages, engaging in conversations, and providing helpful advice and information.

Businesses should also use social media to create content that is relevant to their industry. This can include blog posts, videos, and podcasts. Businesses should use social media to stay up to date with industry trends and news. This is done by following industry leaders and influencers.

Businesses should use social media to measure the success of their campaigns. This is done through tracking likes, comments, and shares. Businesses should use analytics tools to measure the reach and engagement of their posts.

Using social media for business growth and start-ups is a definite process to engage with customers, build relationships, and increase brand awareness. By creating a presence on major social media platforms, engaging with customers, promoting products and services, creating content, and measuring success, businesses can use social media to grow their business and reach new customers.

Video conferencing to connect with remote teams.

Video conferencing is a technology that enables people to communicate with each other over the internet using video and audio. It has become increasingly popular in recent years, as it allows people to stay connected with their colleagues, friends, and family, even when they are not physically present.

- Video conferencing can be used to connect remote teams, allowing them to collaborate on projects, share ideas, and stay up to date on the latest developments. It can also be used for remote training and education, as well as for virtual meetings and conferences. With the help of video conferencing, businesses can save time and money by eliminating the need for travel, while still allowing for productive and efficient communication.

- Video conferencing has become an increasingly popular way for businesses to connect with remote teams and facilitate collaboration. It has become an invaluable tool for businesses of all sizes, from small start-ups to large corporations. Video conferencing offers a number of benefits that can help businesses grow and succeed.

- The most obvious benefit of video conferencing is the ability to connect with remote teams. This allows businesses to collaborate with teams that are located in different parts of the world, without having to travel. This can save businesses time and money, as well as allow them to access a larger pool of talent.

- Video conferencing also allows businesses to stay connected with their teams, even when they are not physically present. This can help to maintain morale and ensure that everyone is on the same page. It also allows businesses to stay in touch with their customers and partners, which can help to build relationships and foster trust.

- Video conferencing can also help businesses to save money. By using video conferencing, businesses can reduce their travel costs and save on the cost of renting meeting rooms. This can help businesses to save money, which can then be reinvested in other areas of the business.

- Video conferencing can also help businesses to increase their productivity. By allowing teams to collaborate remotely, businesses can get more done in less time. This can help businesses to increase their output and improve their bottom line.

- Video conferencing helps businesses stay competitive. By staying connected with their teams and customers, businesses can stay ahead of the competition and ensure that they are providing the best service possible.

Video conferencing is an invaluable tool for businesses of all sizes. It can help businesses to save money, increase productivity, and stay connected with their teams and customers. This can help businesses to grow and succeed.

Project management software to manage tasks and deadlines.

Project management software is a powerful tool for businesses and start-ups to manage tasks and deadlines. It helps to streamline processes, increase efficiency, and improve collaboration. It helps to save time and money by reducing the need for manual processes and ensuring that tasks are completed on time.

- Project management software helps businesses and start-ups to plan and execute projects more efficiently. It is to create a timeline for tasks and deadlines, assign tasks to team members, and track progress to ensure that projects are completed on time and within budget.

- Project management software is to improve collaboration between team members. It also provides a central platform for communication and collaboration, allowing team members to easily share ideas and work together. This helps to reduce the amount of time spent on manual processes and increases efficiency.

- Project management software is to improve customer satisfaction. It is to ensure that customer requests are handled quickly and efficiently, and that customer feedback is taken into account to improve customer loyalty and increase customer satisfaction.

project management software helps to improve business growth and start-ups to identify areas of improvement and ensure that projects are completed on time and within budget. This is to increase profits and ensure that businesses and start-ups are successful.

E-commerce solutions to streamline sales.

E-commerce solutions are becoming increasingly popular for businesses of all sizes, from large corporations to small start-ups. These solutions provide businesses with a range of benefits, including increased efficiency, cost savings, and improved customer service. They also help businesses to streamline their sales processes, allowing them to focus more on growing their business.

- E-commerce solutions help businesses to streamline their sales processes by automating many of the tasks associated with sales. This includes automating order processing, customer service, and inventory management.

- Automation helps to reduce the amount of time and effort required to manage sales, freeing up resources to focus on other areas of the business. Automation helps to ensure accuracy and consistency in the sales process, reducing the chances of errors or missed opportunities.

- E-commerce solutions also help to improve customer service. By automating customer service tasks. Businesses provide customers with faster and more efficient service. This helps to increase customer satisfaction and loyalty, leading to increased sales and revenue. Automated customer service can help to reduce the amount of time and effort required to respond to customer inquiries, freeing up resources to focus on other areas of the business.

E-commerce solutions help businesses to save money. By automating many of the tasks associated with sales, businesses can reduce their overhead costs. This helps to increase profits and allows businesses to reinvest those profits into other areas of the business.

Mobile applications to increase customer engagement.

Mobile applications are becoming increasingly popular for businesses as a way to engage with their customers and increase their growth. Mobile apps can be used to provide customers with a more personalized experience, offer exclusive deals, and provide real-time updates on products and services. They can also be used to collect data about customer behavior and preferences, which can be used to create targeted marketing campaigns.

- The use of mobile applications to increase customer engagement and business growth has been proven to be effective. Studies have shown that businesses that use mobile apps to engage with their customers have seen an increase in customer loyalty and satisfaction, as well as an increase in sales. Businesses that use mobile apps to collect customer data have seen an increase in their ability to target their marketing campaigns and increase their ROI.

- start-ups also benefit from the use of mobile applications to increase customer engagement and business growth. By using mobile apps, start-ups quickly build a customer base and increase their visibility. Mobile apps are used to collect data about customer behavior and preferences, which can be used to create targeted marketing campaigns and increase sales.

Mobile applications are an influential way for businesses to engage with their customers and increase their growth. They are used to provide customers with a more personalized experience, offer exclusive deals, and provide real-time updates on products and services.

Virtual reality to create immersive customer experiences.

Virtual reality (VR) is a technology that allows users to interact with and experience a simulated environment. It has become increasingly popular in recent years, as it has been used to create immersive customer experiences that have a profound impact on business growth and start-ups.

- VR is used to create a unique and engaging customer experience. For example, businesses can use VR to create virtual showrooms, allowing customers to explore products in a realistic, 3D environment. This can be used to provide customers with a more interactive and engaging shopping experience, as well as to provide customers with a better understanding of the product. This helps to increase customer engagement and loyalty, as well as to increase sales.

VR can also be used to create virtual training and educational experiences. This is used to provide customers with a more immersive and engaging learning experience, as well as to provide businesses with a more efficient and cost-effective way to train their employees. This helps to improve employee performance and productivity, as well as to reduce training costs.

Big data to gain insights into customer behavior.

Big data is a term used to describe the large amount of data that is generated by businesses and organizations. It is data that is too large and complex to be processed and analyzed using traditional methods. Big data can be used to gain insights into customer behavior and its impact on business growth and start-ups.

- Big data can be used to identify customer preferences and trends, which can then be used to create targeted marketing campaigns and strategies. By analyzing customer data, businesses can gain insights into customer buying patterns, which are used to better understand customer needs and preferences. This helps businesses to create more effective marketing campaigns and strategies that are tailored to the needs of their customers.

- Big data is also be used to identify potential opportunities for business growth and expansion. By analyzing customer data, businesses identify areas of potential growth and develop strategies to capitalize on those opportunities. This helps businesses to increase their market share and profitability and also reduce their exposure to potential risks and ensure their long-term success.

Big data is used to identify potential areas for innovation. By analyzing customer data, businesses identify areas where new products or services could be developed to meet customer needs for the businesses to stay ahead of the competition and remain competitive in the market.

Voice recognition technology to automate processes.

Voice recognition technology is a rapidly growing technology that is being used to automate processes in businesses and start-ups. This technology is used to recognize and interpret spoken words, allowing users to interact with their devices and applications without the need for manual input. Voice recognition technology has the potential to revolutionize the way businesses and start-ups operate, as it can help to streamline processes, reduce costs, and increase efficiency.

- The most common use of voice recognition technology is in customer service. By using voice recognition technology, businesses provide customers with faster and more accurate responses to their queries to reduce customer wait times and improve customer satisfaction. Voice recognition technology can be used to automate processes such as order processing, payment processing, and customer support to reduce the amount of time and resources required to complete these tasks, allowing businesses to focus on more important tasks.

Voice recognition technology is used to improve the accuracy of data entry. By using voice recognition technology, businesses reduce the amount of time and resources required to enter data into their systems to reduce errors and improve accuracy, resulting in more accurate data and better decision-making.

Machine learning to automate tasks and processes.

Machine learning (ML) is a form of artificial intelligence (AI) that enables computers to learn from data and use it to make decisions. It is a powerful tool that is used to automate tasks and processes, and its impact on business growth and start-ups is immense.

- ML is used to automate many of the tedious and time-consuming tasks that are associated with running a business. For example, ML is used to automate customer service tasks such as responding to customer inquiries, processing orders, and managing customer accounts. ML is also used to automate marketing tasks such as segmenting customers, targeting campaigns, and analyzing customer behavior.

- ML is also used to automate processes such as production, inventory management, and supply chain management. By using ML, businesses reduce costs, increase efficiency, and improve customer satisfaction.

ML is also be used to improve decision-making. By analyzing data, ML identifies patterns and trends that are used to inform decisions for businesses to make better decisions about marketing, product development, and customer service and help businesses increase customer loyalty and retention.

Blockchain technology to secure data and transactions.

Blockchain technology is a revolutionary new way of securing data and transactions. It is a distributed ledger technology that uses cryptography to store and transmit data securely. Blockchain technology has the potential to revolutionize the way businesses operate and grow, as well as how start-ups develop and succeed.

- Blockchain technology is used to securely store and transmit data, such as customer information, financial transactions, and other sensitive information. It is a decentralized system, meaning that it is not controlled by any single entity, making it more secure than traditional systems. Blockchain technology is immutable, meaning that once data is stored on the blockchain, it cannot be changed or altered. This makes it an ideal solution for businesses that need to store and transmit sensitive data securely.

- Blockchain technology is used to facilitate secure transactions by using smart contracts, businesses can create digital contracts that are stored on the blockchain and are executed automatically when certain conditions are met. This eliminates the need for manual verification and reduces the risk of fraud. Blockchain technology is used to create digital tokens that are used to facilitate payments and other transactions. This is especially useful for start-ups that need to quickly and securely process payments.

Blockchain technology is used to create new business models and opportunities for start-ups and businesses that can use blockchain technology to create new products and services, such as decentralized applications (dApps) and decentralized autonomous organizations (DAOs). These new business models open up new markets and create new sources of revenue for businesses and start-ups to reach new heights of success

3D printing to create prototypes and products.

3D printing is a revolutionary technology that has been gaining popularity in recent years. It is a process of creating three-dimensional objects from a digital file using additive manufacturing techniques. 3D printing has been used to create prototypes and products for a variety of industries, including automotive, aerospace, medical, and consumer products.

- The use of 3D printing for prototyping and product development has had a significant impact on business growth and start-ups. By using 3D printing, businesses can quickly and cost-effectively create prototypes and products that are tested and refined before going into production. This allows businesses to get their products to market faster, reducing the time and cost associated with traditional manufacturing methods.

- 3D printing also allows businesses to create custom products that are tailored to the needs of their customers. This allows businesses to create unique products that are sold at a premium price, increasing their profits.

- 3D printing is also used to create parts and components that are difficult or impossible to produce using traditional manufacturing methods for businesses to reduce costs and increase efficiency, resulting in increased profits.

3D printing is used to create products that are more environmentally friendly so that businesses can reduce their reliance on traditional materials and create products that are more sustainable for businesses to reduce their environmental impact and increase their sustainability.

Robotics to automate manufacturing processes.

Robotics is a rapidly growing field that is revolutionizing the manufacturing industry. Robotics is being used to automate processes, reduce costs, and increase efficiency. Robotics has the potential to revolutionize the way businesses operate and grow, as well as create new opportunities for start-ups.

- Robotics can be used to automate processes in manufacturing, such as assembly, packaging, and sorting. Automation reduces labor costs, increases efficiency, and improves product quality. Automation also reduces the need for manual labor, freeing up resources to focus on other areas of the business and reducing the risk of human error, leading to fewer defects and higher customer satisfaction.

- Robotics is used to improve the accuracy and speed of production which are used to monitor and control production processes, ensuring that products are produced with the highest quality and accuracy. Robotics are used to monitor and analyze data, allowing businesses to make more informed decisions and improve their operations.

- Robotics are used to improve customer service and be used to automate customer service tasks, such as responding to customer inquiries, taking orders, and processing payments. This reduces the time and cost associated with customer service, leading to improved customer satisfaction.

Robotics are used to improve safety in the workplace to monitor and control hazardous environments, reducing the risk of accidents and injuries, to monitor and controlling dangerous machinery, ensuring that it is operated safely and efficiently.

Augmented reality to create interactive customer experiences.

Augmented reality (AR) is a technology that allows users to interact with digital content in the physical world. It has the potential to revolutionize the way businesses interact with customers and create interactive experiences. AR is used to create immersive and engaging experiences that help businesses grow and start-ups stand out from the competition.

- AR is used to create interactive experiences that are tailored to the customer's needs. For example, a retail store can use AR to allow customers to virtually try on clothes or accessories before they buy them. This helps customers make informed decisions and increase the likelihood of a purchase. AR is also used to create interactive experiences that are tailored to the customer's interests. For example, a restaurant can use AR to allow customers to explore the menu and learn more about the dishes before they order. One more example is a hotel that can use AR to create a virtual tour of the hotel and its amenities for customers to get a better understanding of the hotel and its services, and make them more likely to book a stay.

- AR is also used to create an interactive experience that allows customers to explore the company's products and services and help customers get a better understanding of the company and its offerings, and make them more likely to invest in the start-up.

Augmented reality has the potential to revolutionize the way businesses interact with customers and create interactive experiences with immersive and engaging experiences

IoT to monitor and control devices remotely.

The Internet of Things (IoT) is a rapidly growing technology that is revolutionizing the way businesses operate. IoT is the network of physical objects, such as devices, vehicles, and buildings, that are connected to the Internet and can collect and exchange data. IoT devices are used to monitor and control devices remotely, allowing businesses to gain insights into their operations and make better decisions. This technology has the potential to drive business growth and create new opportunities for start-ups

- IoT has the potential to drive business growth by providing businesses with real-time data and insights into their operations. By connecting devices and systems, businesses gain insights into their operations and make better decisions. For example, businesses can use IoT to monitor their inventory levels, track customer trends, and optimize their supply chain. IoT can also be used to automate processes and reduce costs, allowing businesses to become more efficient and competitive.

- IoT has the potential to create new opportunities for start-ups. By connecting devices and systems, start-ups develop innovative products and services that are used to improve customer experience and drive business growth.

While IoT has the potential to drive business growth and create new opportunities for start-ups, there are also challenges and opportunities associated with it. Security is a major concern, as IoT devices are vulnerable to cyberattacks as there are privacy concerns associated with the collection and use of data.

Artificial intelligence to automate customer service.

Artificial Intelligence (AI) is a rapidly growing technology that is revolutionizing the way businesses interact with customers. AI-powered customer service automation is becoming increasingly popular among businesses and start-ups, as it offers a more efficient and cost-effective way to provide customer service. AI-powered customer service automation helps businesses and start-ups to improve customer satisfaction, reduce costs, and increase revenue.

- AI-powered customer service automation is used to automate customer service tasks such as responding to customer inquiries, providing customer support, and handling customer complaints to provide personalized customer service experiences by using natural language processing (NLP) to understand customer queries and provide relevant responses. AI-powered customer service automation is also be used to automate customer service processes such as order processing, payment processing, and customer onboarding.

The use of AI-powered customer service automation helps businesses and start-ups to improve customer satisfaction by providing faster and more accurate customer service to reduce costs by automating customer service tasks, which helps to reduce the need for manual labor and to increase revenue by providing personalized customer service experiences and also increasing customer loyalty.

Predictive analytics to anticipate customer needs.

Predictive analytics is a powerful tool that helps businesses anticipate customer needs and make better decisions. It uses data-driven insights to identify patterns and trends in customer behavior, enabling businesses to anticipate customer needs and make decisions that will lead to increased sales and customer satisfaction. Predictive analytics can also be used to identify opportunities for growth and innovation, helping start-ups to stay ahead of the competition.

- Predictive analytics are used to identify customer preferences and anticipate customer needs. By analyzing customer data, businesses can identify patterns in customer behavior and use this information to create targeted marketing campaigns and product offerings to better understand their customers and create more personalized experiences.

- Predictive analytics is also used to identify opportunities for growth and innovation by identifying areas of potential growth and developing strategies to capitalize on them to stay ahead of the competition and increase their market share.

Predictive analytics is used to identify potential risks and opportunities. By analyzing customer data, businesses can identify potential risks and develop strategies to mitigate them and reduce their risk exposure and increase their profitability.

Natural language processing to understand customer queries.

Natural language processing (NLP) is a branch of artificial intelligence that deals with understanding and interpreting human language. It is used to analyze text, speech, and other forms of natural language. NLP is used in a variety of applications, including customer service, search engine optimization, and automated customer support.

- NLP is used to understand customer queries and provide better customer service to gain insights into customer needs and preferences to help businesses tailor their products and services to better meet customer needs. NLP is used to identify customer sentiment, which helps businesses better understand customer satisfaction.

- NLP is used to improve search engine optimization (SEO). By analyzing customer queries, businesses can identify keywords and phrases that are used in customer queries and optimize their content for those terms for businesses to rank higher in search engine results, resulting in more traffic and potential customers.

NLP is used to automate customer support. By analyzing customer queries, businesses can create automated responses that can provide customers with answers to their questions to save time and money by reducing the need for manual customer support. Businesses can identify areas where customers are having difficulty and address those issues to improve customer satisfaction, and loyalty and saves time and money.

Facial recognition technology to improve security.

Facial recognition technology is a rapidly emerging technology that is being used to improve security and business development for small businesses and start-ups. This technology uses facial recognition algorithms to identify individuals based on their facial features. It is being used in a variety of industries, including retail, banking, healthcare, and government.

- Facial recognition technology is used to improve security by providing an additional layer of authentication for access to sensitive areas or data. This is also used to identify potential threats or suspicious activity, such as unauthorized access to a building or computer system, and to identify customers or employees in order to provide personalized services or to track their activities.

By using facial recognition technology, businesses identify potential customers and target them with personalized marketing campaigns to increase customer engagement and loyalty to increase sales.

Digital wallets to facilitate payments.

Digital wallets are becoming increasingly popular as a way to facilitate payments for small businesses and start-ups. Digital wallets allow businesses to accept payments quickly and securely, without the need for cash or credit cards. This makes it easier for customers to make payments and can help businesses to increase their sales and grow their customer base.

- The use of digital wallets helps small businesses and start-ups to reduce the costs associated with processing payments. Using digital wallets, businesses avoid the fees associated with traditional payment methods, such as credit cards and cash which help businesses to save money on transaction fees, which can be used to invest in other areas of the business.

- Digital wallets also make it easier for businesses to track their sales and customer data. By using digital wallets, businesses can easily access customer information and track sales in real-time to help businesses to better understand their customers and make more informed decisions about their business.

Digital wallets also provide businesses with more security. Businesses protect their customers' data and ensure that their payments are secure to help businesses to build trust with their customers to increase their customers.

Virtual assistants to automate customer service.

In the modern world, customer service is a critical component of any business. It is the key to customer satisfaction and loyalty, and it can make or break a business. As such, businesses of all sizes are investing in virtual assistants to automate customer service and improve their customer experience. Virtual assistants are AI-powered chatbots that can handle customer inquiries, provide support, and even process orders. They are becoming increasingly popular among small businesses and start-ups as a cost-effective way to provide customer service

- Virtual assistants offer a range of benefits to small businesses and start-ups. They help to reduce costs, improve customer service, and increase efficiency. Virtual assistants are a cost-effective way to provide customer service. They require no additional staff and can be set up quickly and easily. This can help to reduce overhead costs and free up resources for other areas of the business.

- Virtual assistants provide 24/7 customer service, which can help to improve customer satisfaction and loyalty. They are also customized to provide personalized service and can be programmed to answer common customer questions.

- Virtual assistants automate mundane tasks, such as order processing and customer inquiries to free up resources and allow staff to focus on more important tasks.

Virtual assistants have a positive impact on business development for small businesses and start-ups. They help to reduce costs, improve customer service, and increase efficiency. This led to increased sales, higher customer satisfaction, and improved brand recognition.

Data visualization tools to gain insights

Data visualization is a powerful tool for gaining insights from data and has become increasingly popular in recent years. It is used to present data in a visual format, making it easier to understand and interpret. Data visualization is used to identify trends, spot outliers, and gain insights into customer behavior.

- Data visualization tools are used by small businesses and start-ups to gain insights into their customer base, market trends, and product performance. Visualizing data, businesses quickly identify areas of opportunity and potential risks to help them make better decisions and develop strategies to increase sales and profits.

- Data visualization tools are used to monitor customer engagement and track customer feedback. This can help businesses understand what their customers are looking for and how they can improve their products and services. Data visualization tools are used to analyze customer data and identify areas of improvement.

- Data visualization tools are also used to identify potential areas of growth. By visualizing data, businesses quickly identify opportunities for expansion and identify new markets to target. This helps them develop strategies to increase their customer and increase their revenues.

Data visualization tools are also used to track customer behavior and identify customer segments. This help businesses understand their customers better and develop targeted marketing campaigns. Additionally, data visualization tools can be used to identify customer trends and develop strategies to capitalize on them.

CHAPTER THIRTEEN

Develop a Customer Service Strategy

Customer service is an essential part of any business, regardless of size. It is the foundation of customer loyalty and satisfaction, and it can have a significant impact on the success of a small business or start-up. Developing a customer service strategy is an important step in ensuring that customers have a positive experience with your business.

- The first step in developing a customer service strategy is to identify the goals of the strategy. What do you want to achieve with your customer service strategy? Do you want to increase customer satisfaction? Increase customer loyalty? Increase sales? Identifying your goals will help you develop a strategy that is tailored to your business and its needs.

- Once you have identified your goals, the next step is to create a customer service team. This team should be composed of individuals who have the skills and experience necessary to provide excellent customer service. It is important to ensure that the team is well-trained and knowledgeable about your products and services. It is important to ensure that the team is equipped with the necessary tools and resources to provide effective customer service.

- Once you have created a customer service team, the next step is to develop a process for providing customer service. This process should include steps for responding to customer inquiries, resolving customer complaints, and providing feedback. It should include steps for tracking customer satisfaction and resolving any issues that arise.

In addition to developing a process for providing customer service, it is important to develop a communication plan. This plan should include strategies for communicating with customers, such as email, phone, and social media. It should also include strategies for responding to the customer queries.

CHAPTER FOURTEEN

Create a Network of Partners and Vendors

Creating a network of partners and vendors for small businesses and start-ups is a critical step in the success of any business. Having a strong network of partners and vendors can help a business to grow and succeed. It provides access to resources, contacts, and expertise that can be invaluable. Here are some tips on how to create a network of partners and vendors for small businesses and start-ups.

- **Identify Your Needs**: Before you start building your network, it is important to identify your needs. What type of partners and vendors do you need? What type of services do you need? What type of expertise do you need? Knowing what you need will help you to narrow down your search and make it easier to find the right partners and vendors.

- **Research Potential Partners and Vendors**: Once you have identified your needs, it is time to start researching potential partners and vendors. Look for companies that offer services and expertise that match your needs. Check out their websites, read reviews, and talk to other businesses that have used their services.

- **Reach Out**: Once you have identified potential partners and vendors, it is time to reach out. Contact them and explain what you need and why you think they would be a good fit. Ask questions and be sure to listen to their answers.

- **Negotiate Terms**: Once you have found the right partners and vendors, it is time to negotiate terms. Make sure you understand the terms of the agreement and that you are comfortable with them.

- **Build Relationships**: Once you have established the terms of the agreement, it is important to build relationships with your partners and vendors. Take the time to get to know them and their business. This will help to ensure that you have a strong, long-term relationship.

CHAPTER FIFTEEN

Develop a System for Tracking Progress

Tracking progress is an important part of any business, especially for small businesses and start-ups in order to measure their success and identify areas for improvement.

- **Identify Goals:** The first step in developing a system for tracking progress is to identify the company's goals to ensure that the system is tailored to the specific needs of the business. Goals should be specific, measurable, achievable, realistic, and time-bound.

- **Establish Metrics**: Once the goals have been identified, the next step is to establish metrics that can be used to measure progress toward those goals. These metrics should be chosen based on the goals and should be measurable and actionable.

- **Identify Key Performance Indicators:** It is important to identify key performance indicators (KPIs) that will be used to measure progress. KPIs should be chosen based on the goals that have been set and should be used to track progress over time.

- **Establish a Reporting System**: Once KPIs have been identified, it is important to establish a reporting system that will be used to track progress. This system should include regular reports that are generated on a regular basis, such as weekly or monthly. These reports should include data on the KPIs that have been identified and should be used to measure progress over time.

- **Set up a Tracking System:** The next step is to set up a tracking system. This can be done using a spreadsheet or a software program. The tracking system should include the metrics that have been established and should be updated regularly.

- **Monitor Progress:** Once the tracking system has been set up, it is important to monitor progress regularly. This can be done by reviewing the tracking system on a regular basis and making adjustments as needed.

- **Take Action:** Once progress has been monitored, it is important to take action to ensure that the goals are being met. This can include making changes to the business model, adjusting the KPIs, or implementing new strategies. Taking action is essential to ensure that the business is on track to reach its goals.

- **Make Adjustments:** If the tracking system indicates that progress is not being made, it is important to make adjustments. This could include changing the goals, metrics, or tracking system.

Developing a system for tracking progress is an important part of running a successful business, especially for small businesses and start-ups. This report has outlined the steps necessary to do so.

CHAPTER SIXTEEN

Create a System for Managing Risk

Small businesses and start-ups are often faced with a variety of risks that can have a significant impact on their operations. Managing these risks can be a difficult and time-consuming task, but it is essential for the success of the business. This report outlines a system for managing risk for small businesses and start-ups.

- **Identify the risks:** The first step in creating a system for managing risk for small businesses and start-ups is to identify the risks associated with the business. This includes identifying potential risks such as financial, operational, legal, and environmental risks. Once the risks have been identified, they can be categorized and prioritized based on their potential impact on the business.

- **Assess the risks:** Once the risks have been identified, the next step is to assess the risks. This involves evaluating the potential impact of the risks and determining the likelihood of the risks occurring, the probability of the risk occurring, the severity of the potential impact, and the cost of mitigating the risk. This analysis will help to identify which risks need to be addressed first and which can be managed with a lower priority.

- **Develop a risk management plan:** Once the risks have been identified and assessed, the next step is to develop a risk management plan. This plan should include strategies for mitigating the risks, such as developing policies and procedures, implementing controls, and establishing a risk management team.

- **Implement the risk management plan:** After the risk management plan has been developed, the next step is to implement the plan. This involves putting the plan into action, such as developing policies and procedures, implementing controls, and establishing a risk management team. The plan should also include measures to monitor the risk and ensure that it is being managed effectively.

- **Monitor and review the risk management plan:** Once the risk management plan has been implemented, the next step is to monitor and review the plan. This can be done by regularly reviewing the risk assessment and risk analysis, as well as monitoring the implementation of the risk mitigation plan. This will help to ensure that the risk is being managed effectively and that any changes in the risk environment are being addressed.

- **Communicate the risk management plan:** The final step in creating a system for managing risk for small businesses and start-ups is to communicate the risk management plan. This involves making sure that all stakeholders are aware of the plan and understand their roles and responsibilities.

CHAPTER SEVENTEEN

Develop a System for Managing Customer Relationships

Here we are talking about the steps to develop a system for managing customer relationships for small businesses and start-ups. We outline the key features of the system, the benefits of using the system, and the potential challenges that may arise during the development process.

The system for managing customer relationships should include the following key features:

- The customer database stores customer information such as contact details, preferences, and purchase history.

- Customer relationship management (CRM) system that allows businesses to track customer interactions and build relationships with customers.

- Customer service system that enables businesses to respond quickly to customer inquiries and complaints.

- Marketing automation system that allows businesses to create and manage campaigns, track customer engagement, and measure the effectiveness of campaigns.

- An analytics system that allows businesses to track customer behavior and identify trends.

A system for managing customer relationships will provide the following benefits to small businesses and start-ups:

- **Improved customer service**: The system will enable businesses to respond quickly to customer inquiries and complaints, resulting in improved customer satisfaction.

- **Increased customer loyalty**: The system will allow businesses to track customer interactions and build relationships with customers, resulting in increased customer loyalty.

- **Increased sales**: The system will enable businesses to create and manage campaigns, track customer engagement, and measure the effectiveness of campaigns, resulting in increased sales.

- **Improved decision-making**: The system will allow businesses to track customer behavior and identify trends, resulting in improved decision-making.

Developing a system for managing customer relationships will have the following potential challenges:

- **Cost**: The cost of developing the system may be prohibitive for some small businesses and start-ups.

- **Complexity:** The system may be complex to implement and manage, requiring specialized knowledge and resources.

- **Security**: The system must be secure to protect customer data from unauthorized access.

The system for managing customerrelationships will enable businesses to improve customer service, increase customer loyalty, increase sales, and improve decision-making. The development of the system may be subject to potential challenges such as cost, complexity, and security.

CHAPTER EIGHTEEN

Develop a System for Managing Employee Relationships

Employee relationships are an important part of any business, especially for small businesses and start-ups. A good system for managing employee relationships can help to ensure that employees are happy and productive and that the business is running smoothly. Here are a few points for managing employee relationships for small businesses and start-ups.

- Improve communication between employees and management.

- Create a positive work environment.

- Foster trust and respect between employees and management.

- Increase employee engagement and productivity.

- Reduce employee turnover.

The system for managing employee relationships for small businesses and start-ups should include the following components:

- **Open Communication**: Establishing open lines of communication between employees and management is essential. This can be done through regular meetings, feedback sessions, and surveys.

- **Employee Recognition**: Recognizing and rewarding employees for their hard work and dedication are important for creating a positive work environment. This can be done through awards, bonuses, and other incentives.

- **Training and Development**: Providing employees with the necessary training and development opportunities is key to fostering trust and respect between employees and management. This can be done through workshops, seminars, and other learning opportunities.

- **Employee Engagement**: Encouraging employees to be engaged in their work is important for increasing productivity. This can be done through team-building activities, social events, and other activities.

- **Performance Management**: Establishing a system for performance management is essential for ensuring that employees are meeting their goals and objectives. This can be done through regular performance reviews and feedback sessions.

A system for managing employee relationships for small businesses and start-ups is essential for ensuring that employees are happy and productive and that the business is running smoothly. This outlines a system for managing employee relationships for small businesses and start-ups that includes open communication, employee recognition, training and development, employee engagement, and performance management. Implementing this system helps to improve communication, create a positive work environment, foster trust, and respect, increase employee engagement and productivity, reduce employee turnover, and improve customer service.

CHAPTER NINETEEN

Create a System for Managing Inventory

Small businesses and start-ups often struggle with managing their inventory. Without the right system in place, it can be difficult to keep track of what is in stock, what needs to be ordered, and when items need to be restocked. The points outlines a system for managing inventory for small businesses and start-ups that is cost-effective, easy to use, and efficient.

The first step in creating an inventory management system is to determine the most cost-effective solution. For small businesses and start-ups, this often means using existing software or hardware that is already available. For example, cloud-based software's can be used to track inventory levels, orders, and sales. Barcode scanners and RFID readers can be used to quickly and accurately track inventory levels.

The next step is to ensure that the system is easy to use. This means that the software or hardware should be intuitive and user-friendly. The system should be able to integrate with existing systems and processes, such as accounting software or point-of-sale systems.

The system should be efficient. This means that it should be able to quickly and accurately track inventory levels, orders, and sales. The system should be able to generate reports and alerts when inventory levels are low or when items need to be restocked.

Creating a system for managing inventory for small businesses and start-ups is essential for success. By utilizing cost-effective solutions, ensuring that the system is easy to use, and making sure that it is efficient, businesses can ensure that their inventory is properly managed.

CHAPTER TWENTY

Managing Customer Feedback

Customer feedback is an invaluable asset for small businesses and start-ups. It provides valuable insights into customer satisfaction, product quality, and customer service. By managing customer feedback effectively, businesses identify areas for improvement and take the necessary steps to ensure customer satisfaction.

The following are some tips for managing customer feedback for small businesses and start-ups:

Establish a System for Collecting Customer Feedback:

The first step in managing customer feedback is to establish a system for collecting customer feedback. This could include surveys, customer service calls, online reviews, or other methods.

Methods to collect customer feedback

- **Surveys:** Surveys are one of the most popular ways to collect customer feedback. Surveys can be distributed online or in person and can be used to collect feedback on a variety of topics, such as customer satisfaction, product or service quality, and customer experience.

- **Focus Groups:** Focus groups are a great way to get direct customer feedback. Focus groups involve gathering a small group of customers together to discuss a particular product or service. This type of feedback can be invaluable for understanding customer needs and preferences.

- **Interviews:** Interviews are another great way to collect customer feedback. Interviews can be conducted in person or over the phone and can be used to gain a better understanding of customer needs and preferences.

- **Online Reviews:** Online reviews are a great way to get customer feedback. Customers can post reviews on websites such as Yelp, Google, and Facebook, which can be used to gain valuable insights into customer experiences.

- **Social Media:** Social media is a great way to collect customer feedback. Customers can post comments and reviews on social media platforms such as Twitter, Facebook, and Instagram, which can be used to gain valuable insights into customer experiences.

- **Customer Service:** Customer service is a great way to collect customer feedback. Customers can provide feedback through customer service channels such as phone, email, and live chat, which can be used to gain valuable insights into customer experiences.

Monitor Customer Feedback Regularly:

Once a system for collecting customer feedback is established, it is important to monitor customer feedback regularly. This will help to identify any trends or patterns in customer feedback that can be addressed.

Respond to Customer Feedback:

Once customer feedback is collected, it is important to respond to it in a timely manner. This could include addressing customer complaints, thanking customers for their feedback, or offering solutions to problems.

Analyze Customer Feedback:

Once customer feedback is collected and responded to, it is important to analyze the feedback to identify any trends or patterns. This will help to identify areas where the business can improve.

Take Action:

Once customer feedback is analyzed, it is important to take action to address any issues that were identified. This could include making changes to products or services, improving customer service, or implementing new policies.

Follow-Up:

Finally, it is important to follow up with customers to ensure that their feedback was addressed and that any changes that were made were effective. This will help to ensure that customers are satisfied with the business and that their feedback is taken seriously.

By following these tips, small businesses and start-ups can effectively manage customer feedback and ensure customer satisfaction. This will help to build customer loyalty and increase sales.

CHAPTER TWENTY-ONE

Develop a System for Managing Customer Data

Small businesses and start-ups have to manage customer data in order to stay competitive and maximize their profits. Customer data is the lifeblood of any business, and it's essential to have a system in place to store and manage this data effectively.

The first step in managing customer data is to collect it. This can be done through a variety of methods, such as surveys, customer feedback forms, and online sign-ups. Once the data is collected, it needs to be stored in a secure database. This can be done using a customer relationship management (CRM) system, which is a software program designed to store and manage customer information.

Once the data is stored, it needs to be organized. This can be done by creating customer profiles, which are detailed records of each customer's information. These profiles can include contact information, purchase history, preferences, and other relevant data.

Once the customer profiles are created, the data needs to be analyzed. This can be done using analytics software, which can help identify trends and patterns in customer behavior. This data can then be used to create targeted marketing campaigns and personalize customer experiences.

Finally, the data needs to be kept up-to-date. This can be done by regularly updating customer profiles and tracking customer interactions. This will ensure that the data is accurate and up-to-date, which is essential for effective marketing and customer service.

Use a Customer Relationship Management (CRM) System:

A CRM system is a great way to manage customer data for small businesses and start-ups. It allows you to store customer information, track customer interactions, and analyze customer data to better understand customer behavior and preferences.

Utilize Social Media:

Social media is a great way to engage with customers and build relationships. It also provides an opportunity to collect customer data such as demographics, interests, and preferences.

Collect Customer Feedback:

Customer feedback is invaluable when it comes to understanding customer needs and preferences. Collecting customer feedback through surveys, polls, and other methods can help you better understand your customers and make informed decisions.

Leverage Automation:

Automation can help you save time and resources when it comes to managing customer data. Automation tools can help you streamline customer data collection, segment customers, and automate customer communications.

Analyze Customer Data:

Analyzing customer data can help you gain valuable insights into customer behavior and preferences. This can help you better understand customer needs and develop strategies to better serve them.

Managing customer data is essential for small businesses and start-ups. By collecting, storing, organizing, analyzing, and updating customer data, businesses can maximize their profits and stay competitive.

Wishing you Happy Business!

Unlock Your Business Potential Now

We hope that this book has been a valuable resource for small business owners and start-ups looking to develop their businesses. We have provided a comprehensive overview of the different aspects of business development, from understanding the market and identifying opportunities to developing a business plan and managing finances. We have also discussed the importance of developing a strong team and creating a culture of innovation.

We wish you the best of luck in your business development journey!

Sincerely,

Sangati Jagan Mohan Reddy

you can reach out to me on

Twitter : @jaganreddyms

Koo : @jmr